MARKETING
BATTLEGROUND

How to Deploy Under-the-Radar
Strategies to Explode Your Profits

KENNY ATCHESON

Colossus Publishing

Copyright © 2015 by Kenny Atcheson

Editing by Heidi Wallenborn

Cover design byDaria Lacy

Special quantity discounts may be available for this title. For bulk purchase questions go to www.ColossusPublishing.com

Publisher Disclaimer

Published in the United States of America
by Colossus Publishing
ISBN: 978-1-941256-03-9

Colossus Publishing is a publisher of non-fiction books authored by thought leaders and entrepreneurs that wish to share their experience, stories, passion, and ideas with the world. If you have a book idea that you would like us to consider for publishing, please request an Info-Pack at www.ColossusPublishing.com

AUTHOR DISCLAIMER

For the purpose of this disclaimer, "the author" is also referring to Kenny Atcheson, his company, representatives, independent agents, and all affiliated businesses.

ACCURACY OF INFORMATION

Every effort has been made to accurately represent the information that is shared here and elsewhere by the author and representatives in print, by phone, webinar, in person, and all other communications. However, there is no guarantee that you will benefit in any way by reading or acting on any of this information, recommendations, or perceived recommendations. The information shared is not to be interpreted as a promise or guarantee in any way. Success is entirely dependent on the person/company using the information, products, ideas and techniques.

INDEMNITY AND ABSENCE OF WARRANTY

The author expressly disclaims all warranties as to the contents of all publications, advice, email, phone calls, articles, videos, and any communication not mentioned here, without limitation, the implied warranties of merchantability, fitness for a particular purpose, infringement, and makes no warranty as to the results that may be achieved by using the information contained in any communication made by the author.

Although the author may create systems, strategies, and/or content on your behalf, you are solely responsible for their use. Rely on your own legal team in situations you deem it necessary. There is no way for the author to keep up with legal issues in every country, state, and city. You accept full and sole responsibility for the use of, accuracy, and legal uses of all information, systems, advice, recommendations, and anything mentioned by the author and indemnify the author against any and all liabilities or costs arising from your use of anything mentioned or provided.

ENDORSEMENTS AND DUE DILIGENCE

On occasion, the author will promote, endorse, or suggest products and/or services for sale. Recommendations are always based on the belief that the product/service will be an excellent value based on a review of that product, relationship with that person or company, and or a positive experience with the person or company's product that is being recommended. In some cases, the author will be compensated with free samples, discounts, or referral commission if you decide to purchase that product based on that recommendation. Please do your own due-diligence before making any purchases.

Table of Contents

ACKNOWLEDGEMENTS

First I would like to thank the Lord for **everything**.

I want to thank my wife for her love and support, especially as I spent long hours researching, prepping, and writing this book.

Thank you to my family, friends, mentors, clients, team, and other supporters. You have all made an important contribution to my life.

PREFACE

When I meet with clients during a consulting day, I point out under-utilized media channels. Together, we also unearth hidden wealth and assets within their business, and look at opportunities to deploy strategies that will maximize those assets.

Many books that I've read, workshops I have attended, and businesses that I've researched, are doing and saying the same things — plus or minus 10 percent. A slew of entrepreneurs who I have met are frustrated and willing to do something different — if they just knew what to do.

My experience during those consulting days, along with what I have read in hundreds of marketing and business books, is what prompted me to write this book.

I want to offer something different.

This book is easy to follow, and the ideas presented are simplified for implementation. There is some technology mentioned but the technophobe should have no fear — it is not a book of technical wizardry.

Much of what is revealed should be helpful to any and all business owners, with slight variations and tweaks to make them work. Some of what I share with you is obviously marketing, but you may be shocked that some of the material I write about is found in a "marketing" book. Part of the content is not always viewed as marketing, but in today's world, I can assure you — it is.

I have made every effort to make this book unique in its content, writing style, and theme. I have used military jargon and themed the entire book after military principles, strategies, and tactics. This is in no way to diminish the military and soldiers everywhere by comparing marketing and business to military efforts and conflict. My intent is just the opposite. I have such a tremendous respect for military personnel; you could say that comparing marketing strategies to military is more of a dedication to their hard work, discipline, and success.

The phrase, "under-the-radar" is used in the title because much of what you will read in this book — if you implement these ideas — will fly under-the-radar of your competition. If you have competitors who are outperforming your business and you can't figure out why, it could be because they are deploying their own under-the-radar strategies. Their success will likely not be highly detectible big media buys and ads that everyone can copy. By launching the stealthy tactics contained within this book, you will leave your competition scratching their heads and feeling like you have the top-secret, classified, blueprints for success.

Throughout this book there are references from one chapter to the next. For this reason, I recommend that you read each chapter in order rather than skipping around.

As the purchaser of this book, you now have special security clearance to the classified files and resources that we have crafted specifically for you on the website built just for you at **KennyTalks.com**

Enjoy the battle,

Kenny Atcheson

CHAPTER 1

Cufflinks and Other Stories

Although it was only the second inning, sweat dripped in rivulets down the side of my face. In Las Vegas, it was 98 degrees on a mid-May morning. I played left field on this particular day for the championship game. Usually I played center field, but the guy who normally played left field was injured. We had another capable center fielder, so I volunteered to play left field — a decision that I later regretted. My choice was life-altering.

The batter hit a sinking line-drive toward the gap between me and the center fielder. I charged in to my left to make the catch. At the last moment I dove, landed on my chest and slid across the grass — just as I had done hundreds of times in my life.

When I was eight years old, my dad taught me how to play baseball. From the beginning he taught me to play all-out, all of the time — never holding back.

I remember a game when Dad and I played softball on the same men's team. He batted second and I batted third. He stood on first base, raring to go when I hit a ball to the right-centerfield fence. Dad came wide around third base, legs pumping hard to score in a race against a throw from the center fielder. He slid in and busted his ankle — in a game that we were winning by 10 runs. We didn't really need that extra run. But that was how he played — all-out, all of the time. That is what he coached and ingrained into me.

The all-out style of play that I learned from Dad led to this life-changing day in May.

When our half-inning ended I came up to bat. I drilled a line drive to the right-centerfield fence. As I raced to third I could see our third base coach, Chris, signal me to keep running and go for an inside-the-park homerun. Chris and I had played together for years, so he knew my speed well and I trusted his base coaching judgment. Yet I stopped at third. Incredulous, Chris said, "What are you doing? I was telling you to go." I panted hard, "I can't breathe. I don't have the energy."

I was completely winded and probably would have collapsed if I had kept running. Little did I know that I would collapse later.

For the next two innings I chased balls all over the outfield. After all, this was softball and outfielders get a lot of action, especially when facing good hitting teams. But all of that action led me to do something I had never done before. My dad would have got on me had he witnessed me doing this as a kid: between batters while in the outfield, I took a knee. I had a hard time standing because I had trouble breathing. My chest hurt like never before. I thought I must have really bruised my sternum or something when I landed hard and slid on my chest. The pain was so severe that I thought, *This is probably what a heart attack feels like.*

After the inning ended I headed to the restaurant that overlooked the field instead of sitting in the dugout as usual. It was air conditioned and I thought cooling down would help me breathe. Eileen, Chris's wife, approached me. Like Chris, she knew me pretty well. She had been coming to our games for years. She was like the Team Mom or the assistant coach in the stands. She cheered for us or yelled at us when we needed it. Eileen sat next to me and said, "Kenny, you don't look right. I need to take you to the hospital." I thanked her for her concern but brushed her off.

The pain continued but I kept playing. In my last at-bat as I stood in the batter's box I thought, *I can barely stand. I am going to swing at the first pitch no matter where it is.* I knocked a base hit into the outfield and stopped at first base. I called for timeout as soon as I got there and asked for a pinch runner. I went straight up to the restaurant for relief. Eileen was still there. This time she was insistent. "Kenny, please let me take you to the hospital. I can see you wiggling your left arm and opening and closing your left hand."

I told Eileen to wait. I knew what she thought. I kept wiggling my left arm. It felt like it was asleep. It felt numb. I had read about this type of sensation and it made no sense for someone like me. I was healthy at 180 pounds, exercised regularly, am a non-smoker with no drug use and enjoyed a fairly good diet. What Eileen never said, but suggested, made no sense in my situation. The game ended while I sat in the restaurant with Eileen. The moment it finished I said, "Okay. Please take me to the hospital."

Eileen jumped into action. She ran and told her husband she was taking me to the hospital and for him to pick her up later and to take my baseball bag. Because I still denied that it could be too serious, I had Eileen drive me to the hospital that was across town but closer to my house. This would make it easier for my wife, Jean, to come to the hospital and take me home.

On the way to the emergency room I lost energy. Eileen thought I was going to pass out so she kept asking random questions trying to keep me conscious. I called my wife and told her I was having chest pain and Eileen was driving me to the hospital. I told her not to worry, no big deal, get to the hospital when she could.

When we arrived I walked up to the front desk. Two women checked people in. I approached the first lady and she said, "Fill out the forms over there and have a seat…" Before she finished talking I said, "I am not filling out anything. I am having chest pain, I can't breathe, and I can barely stand." The second lady watched our interaction, picked up the phone and said something I couldn't quite hear but I thought I caught the words "EKG" and "Stat" but I wasn't sure.

A moment later two people hurried out of the back and took me straight to a hospital bed. I was connected to machinery and they started running tests. Shortly afterward a doctor appeared and said, "Mr. Atcheson, you are having a heart attack."

In disbelief I replied, "Are you sure?"

He said, "Yes," and I was moved in a hurry to another bed. From there, things moved quickly. Now there were six people doing things to me at the same time. They undressed me, put me in a hospital gown, handed my baseball pants and jersey to Eileen, stuck me with needles and hooked me up to monitors. There was so much going on at one time it was like the kind of organized chaos that you see in a movie or television show. As a team they worked fast and hard.

During the chaos a man made his way through the crowd in the room and introduced himself. He said, "I am the hospital priest. Whenever someone is in your situation I come talk to them." Then it hit me — the situation that *I* was in? The priest asked if I believed in God. With clarity, I told the priest that I believed in God and Jesus Christ. That was probably the only thing clear to me at that moment. The priest prayed with me then stepped out of the way as the hospital staff kept working on me.

I started to sweat profusely like I never had before. I had played baseball in 118 degrees before wearing catcher's gear and had never sweated like this. The nurse toweled off my face and seconds later sweat dripped into my eyes again. Yet I was freezing. Muscles in my body that I didn't know existed started to shake uncontrollably. The pain was worse, my energy faded and finally a moment came when I thought, *This is it. The end. I am coming to see you Lord.*

I had an overwhelming sense of peace. I may have even cracked a smile for the first time in a couple of hours. Today I wish there had been a video camera above the hospital bed at that moment so that I can visually see my reaction. I didn't have an out-of-body experience and my heart did not stop, but it was an instant in time that I find difficult to describe.

Suddenly a nurse stuck me with a needle, slapped my face, said my name, or did something to take me out of my moment. Then I prayed. I realized that my wife had not arrived at the hospital yet. I prayed and begged God that if these were my last few minutes, at least let me live until my wife arrives so that I can say goodbye.

A few minutes later my wife was by my side.

Amazingly, my heart attack had been going on for over 90 minutes — maybe even closer to two hours because I had continued to play softball after it started. I was still in the emergency room instead of a Cath Lab because there were two other heart attacks going on when I arrived. The Cath Lab is a sterilized place where heart attack patients are taken in order to have surgery to open up the artery or to remove blockage to get the blood flowing again. Because I lay there for so long and my condition worsened, the medical team decided to do something risky rather than stand around and wait. My wife filled out paperwork prior to this procedure. Later, my wife, Jean, said that she had no idea what she was signing at the time because it all happened so fast and she was panicked.

The medical staff gave me a "clot buster" which thins the blood in hopes of breaking down a clot so that blood can flow normally. It is dangerous to do this prior to going to the Cath Lab because the last thing a surgeon wants is blood thinner in the system before he or she cuts into a main artery. A patient can bleed out.

Finally, a Cath Lab was available. With my frightened wife watching, I was wheeled off to surgery. The next thing I remember is that I could feel something digging in my heart. I groaned and the surgeon said, "You can feel that?" I replied, "Yes. It hurts." He dug around in my heart and inside the artery with a special tool to increase blood flow. It felt strange. Imagine someone with a sharp fingernail poking your heart from the inside.

I woke up in critical care after the surgery. My dad, my wife, my cousin, and my friend Pastor Cody was there. Cody is also a retired nurse. He held up the picture of my heart prior to the surgeon getting the blood flowing again. He said, "Kenny, the only time I have seen a picture of a heart like this, it is from a dead person. God decided that today was not your day."

Details came later of what took place in the Cath Lab prior to my waking up in critical care. The cardiac surgeon had difficulty getting my blood flowing through my artery. They inserted a camera that goes up through the artery to look for blockage. They found an artery completely closed but without any visible blockage. Imagine a drinking straw pinched between your fingers so no liquid gets through. No wonder the clot buster didn't work!

One interesting thing that happened is that a representative from the company that invented the technology that pushed the camera up through the artery was in the Cath Lab. When the surgeon struggled to unblock my artery he looked at the representative and she was as dumbfounded as the surgeon. The heart surgeon finally got a metal tube called a stent inserted into my artery where the blood flow had stopped which allowed blood to flow again. It's a good thing the complications that led to extra time in the operating room didn't cause me to bleed out because I was given a "clot buster" blood thinner prior to surgery. That didn't help.

Due to its uniqueness, my situation was used as an unofficial case study passed around the country. Surgeons were asked if they had ever seen anything like this before.

> *May 2012 Case KCIREVAM: 40-year-old male in good physical condition, non-smoker, non-drug user, only occasional alcohol consumption, athletic, no plaque build-up in arteries, has heart attack with 100% stoppage of blood flow.*

A few surgeons responded with, "Yes, when the person has had trauma to the chest."

> *Case Findings: Patient suffered a rare, trauma-induced heart attack.*

Doctors and surgeons believe that my second inning dive for the ball and subsequent sliding on my chest caused a trauma-induced heart attack.

I left the hospital excited to be at home with my wife and to see my dogs. Jean had to keep them from jumping on me because I had to be careful of the stitches at the artery entrance. It could bust wide open and I could bleed to death. *Great!* I thought. I wasn't allowed to vacuum either because the doctor said it is too much effort and strain on the area. Four days earlier I dove for softballs in the championship game and now I couldn't even vacuum.

Two weeks after my heart attack, Jean came with me to a follow-up visit with Dr. Hanson,* the doctor who oper-

---

*Doctor's name has been changed

ated on me. During my visit he seemed tired and disinterested. He even yawned while I was in the middle of telling him that my heart felt strange and that I had incredible pain in my leg from the complications. My leg suffered internal bleeding during surgery after I was given a blood thinner. It was so painful the leg was later tested for nerve damage.

After that visit my wife and I had doubts about this doctor. He didn't seem to care. But I wasn't ready to jump to another cardiologist. After all, this was the guy who performed a complicated procedure on me just two weeks prior. However, the visit put doubt into our minds. So I did the logical thing…

I went to Google and read what other people had to say about my cardiologist, Dr. Hanson

His online reviews were not good. Past patients made comments about Dr. Hanson that I related to. They told mini-stories about what happened to them and how the doctor treated them. The doctor's aloofness had also bothered others. My next step was to read the online reviews for Dr. Botto,** the cardiologist that a friend had recommended. His online reviews were outstanding. So I made the switch.

It is important for you to understand — I thought I was going to die. Dr. Hanson got my blood flowing through my arteries again. But I still left his care to go to another doctor after reading poor online reviews. My friend's recommendation was not enough for me to leave Dr. Hanson; his aloofness was not enough to leave. BUT when I read several bad online reviews — "See ya!"

**Doctor's name has been changed.

What does my story have to do with the marketing battleground?

In this book you will discover a number of strategies, tactics and ideas; but one thing that should be a major part of *all* of your communications and marketing is — **stories**. Stories can be powerful and engaging. They can be used to soften a sales pitch. Stories can be used to illustrate an important point and help people remember it.

My story can be used to illustrate the six following points:

1 - The importance of online reviews

The negative reviews that I read validated something I already felt. Dr. Hanson's bad day during my first visit led me online to read them. Would the negative reviews alone have caused me to leave the doctor? Probably not. Sometimes all it takes is one misstep to send someone searching for other people's experiences with a business. In this case, the doctor already had my initial business. However, most of the time your potential customer will read about other's experiences with you **before** they give you one dollar.

2 - You need a feedback system

Knowing how your customers feel about their experience is critical. It is a mistake to expect that people will let you know if there is a problem. According to Lee Resource Inc., for every customer who bothers to complain, 26 others remain silent.

When there is a problem, it needs to be corrected. But if you don't know there is a problem in the first place, it can't get corrected. You may not know what's happening unless it is taking place right in front of you. In my case the doctor's poor attitude was the issue, but what if my experience at the front desk or with checking out was the problem? The doctor might never know.

Every organization has points in the process where ownership is unaware of potential issues. An effective feedback system alleviates this problem. It will also help your organization to avoid negative online reviews. If unhappy customers are given a place to vent they will most likely do it through your system instead of going public.

Don't forget about happy customers' feedback. A slew of happy customers may tell you something they love about your business that you didn't think mattered much. Collect positive feedback to share with your team to make them feel appreciated, and to use in your marketing when appropriate.

Chapter 7 has more information about customer feedback. For feedback tools and resources go to **KennyTalks.com**

3 - Customers have access to research

Your customers have more research at their fingertips than ever before. Within seconds, they can find out what others have to say about you and your company. They can also find alternatives to your business within seconds. Even if there is not much information about you online — or it is mediocre — your customer can quickly find a cheaper option. Customer perceptions about you or your industry as a whole really do matter. You need to be unique, not interchangeable — such as a doctor who yawns during an appointment and loses a patient.

4 - Perceptions

If I had been given an opportunity to look for a cardiologist prior to needing surgery I would have researched more.

I would have read online reviews and visited his website. I would have looked at the information through the lens of my own perception. Every industry has its own perceptions bias. Go to Google and type in

why are doctors...

Before you can finish typing, you will get four instant responses from Google — many of which are terrible. I am referring to the drop-down of selections that you see **BEFORE** you hit *search* or *enter*. This isn't Google's opinion. It is public perception. Here is how it works: Google's technology is trying to guess what you are going to type in before you finish typing. That way you can simply click on the question you had started to type into Google without having to finish the entire sentence. Google's drop-down selections are an educated guess of what Google's technology thinks you are going to ask, based on what everyone else types in after using the same first words of that sentence.

I could make the point that some people have the perception that too many doctors don't care enough about the individual patient. People believe that doctors want to get in and out of a room to get to the next patient. Truthfully, perhaps that thought was in the back of my mind when my particular doctor seemed aloof.

5 - Everything matters

My story about what happened with my doctor demonstrates that everything matters. In this example, the doctor's marketing position is his relationship with the hospital. That's good. He has put himself in a place where his customers/patients arrive when they need his services. His initial sale and delivery of service to me with surgery was good. But the service and communication/marketing after the initial "sale" was lacking. If there is no loyalty, you are only as good as your last service.

6 - Communication leads to loyalty

There was plenty of time between my hospital stay and my first follow-up visit at Dr. Hanson's office. Someone in the doctor's office could have sent a card via postal mail that said, *"Glad we were able to get your heart pumping away again. Looking forward to seeing you and helping you stay healthy."* That little touch would have gone a long way. Maybe I would have overlooked his aloofness. A card, newsletter, or handwritten note saying something similar a few days after my uninspiring first in-person visit to the doctor's office may have kept me from doubting whether the doctor really cared. Maybe I would not have researched and found his negative reviews. That personal touch may have been just enough to keep me from considering another doctor. Perhaps I would have gone to a second follow-up visit where he would have been more alert and impressive. A thoughtful deed could have led to many more visits and thousands more dollars in his pocket. Unfortunately, our only communication from his office was when they wanted money or during a poor delivery of services. If your only communication with your customers is when you are taking or asking for their money — don't expect loyalty.

Using stories

If I was selling a seminar, training, product, or service that involved any of the six points just mentioned — I could use the story to make important points. If needed, my story could be shorter or chopped into pieces to fit inside limited space or time. Stories are used a number of ways for a number of reasons.

Television has birthed numerous reality celebrities who simply share stories about their day. Some producers deliberately put regular, everyday people into a setting in which the most compelling stories will evolve. When reality shows are full of real celebrities, their real-life stories are on display.

Movies are all about stories. Blockbuster action movies weave stories *into* the action. Many people, including myself, enjoy the first movie in a superhero series because it includes character building — the story portion of the movie. During the first movie in any series we discover that:

- Superman: Kal-El lived on Krypton, but his planet blew up and he was sent to Earth where he has super powers.

- Spiderman: Peter Parker was a young man living with his aunt and uncle when he was bitten by a radioactive spider.

- Batman: Bruce Wayne was a boy who fell down a hole full of bats. He later became an orphan after criminals murdered his parents. He turned into a billionaire genius who decided to fight crime to exact revenge on criminals.

- The Hulk: Bruce Banner is a scientist who was exposed to unusual amounts of gamma radiation causing him to turn green and powerful when angry.

Human beings are fascinated by stories; science and research support it

Recent breakthroughs in neuroscience show that our brain is hardwired to respond to storytelling; the pleasure we derive from a tale well told is nature's way of seducing us into paying attention to it. [1]

Jessica Marshall's article, "Mind Reading: The Science of Storytelling," in the February 2011 edition of *New Scientist*, suggests that people are addicted to stories. Marshall presents an overview of research studies about the impact that storytelling has on the human brain and emotions. Storytelling evokes a strong neurological response. Neuro-economist Paul Zak's research found that during tense moments in a story our brains produce the stress hormone cortisol which allows us to focus. The cute factor of animals releases oxytocin, which is the feel-good chemical that promotes connection and empathy. With oxytocin and cortisol in play, those who had higher amounts of oxytocin were much more likely to give money to someone they'd never met.[2]

Is it possible to plant ideas into someone's brain like in the movie, *Inception*? Yes. Verbal communication enables us to transport information across brains — independent of the actual situation such as telling a story about past events. This phenomenon may be reflected in the speaker's ability to directly induce similar brain patterns in another person simply by speaking, in the absence of any other stimulation.[3]

Penn State College of Medicine researchers found that medical students' attitudes about dementia patients — who are perceived as difficult to treat — improved substantially after students participated in storytelling exercises that made them more sympathetic to their patients' conditions.[4] There are hundreds more studies and research articles that prove the importance of stories in our lives — and how they can be used for influence and business success.

Specific examples of how stories are used and who uses them:

From the time we are young, fictional stories influence the way that we think. *The Little Engine That Could* is used to influence kids to not give up. You may remember the engine's phrase from elementary school, "*I think I can, I think I can.*"

Product placement in movies and on television shows happens more often than you might think. The best product placement examples come from products that are woven into the middle of a story. Reese's Pieces were used to lure the shy little alien from his hiding place in the 1982 blockbuster *E.T.* The candy saw a reported 65 percent jump in profits just two weeks after the movie's premiere.[5]

Most people can recall details from stories about Noah, Moses, and David and Goliath even if they don't read the Bible. People probably remember details from those stories more than they can remember the Ten Commandments.

When my mom died, I wanted to speak at her funeral although I knew it would be difficult. I speak for a living, so I figured I could get through it. My sister wanted to speak on stage at our mom's funeral right after I spoke. However, she had never spoken in front of a group before and was understandably nervous. As her big brother I wanted to coach her because I do a considerable amount of speaking myself. However, this was not a normal first speaking gig. So I told my sister, "Think of a funny story that will remind people of Mom's personality and tell it." She told a great story, everybody laughed. Her speech with her story was a hit.

Abraham Lincoln is recognized as one of the best communicators of all the United States presidents. *Through his hundreds of public speeches, uncanny storytelling ability and the authorship of thousands of letters, he mastered the art of effective communication.*[6]

Disciples asked questions, so Jesus told stories to teach valuable lessons. In the same way, you can tell stories that allow the listener (your customers) to make the connection on their own, which is more powerful than you telling them directly.

Proctor & Gamble, a company with net sales in excess of $83 billion in 2014, employs a Corporate Storyteller. P&G is a consumer product company that puts out multitudes of story-driven advertising campaigns. (PG Annual Report 2014)

Widely considered to be one of the most successful advertisements of all time is a story-based advertisement from the *Wall Street Journal.* The ad generated an estimated $2 billion in revenue.[7]

The story is about two young men who graduated from the same college. The ad explains how they are similar. They returned to college for their 25th reunion and were still very much alike. But there was a difference: one man was manager of a small department in a company; the other was its president. The ad explains that the difference was in what each person knew and how he made use of his knowledge — and that the whole purpose of the *Wall Street Journal* is to give readers knowledge that they can use in business.

During a full day of consultation with clients I sometimes tell the story about Claude Hopkins' work with Schlitz beer in the early 1900s. Schlitz was losing market share and Claude was hired to save the day — and he did. To paraphrase: Hopkins met with Schlitz officials and wanted to know everything about the beer and the beer-making process. It is likely that Schlitz representatives didn't know why the advertising expert and author of *Scientific Advertising* was so inquisitive about how to make beer. Nevertheless, they treated Hopkins to a tour of the brewery. Once Hopkins was aware of all of the work that went into making beer he asked, "Why isn't this part of your advertising?" Hopkins was told that much of the process was similar to other beer manufacturers. However, Hopkins pointed out, "The public doesn't know that." So he created an ad that told the following:

"All beer is cooled in a plate glass room in filtered air."

"Then the beer is filtered."

"Then it is sterilized after being bottled and sealed."

Hopkins' ad didn't just say that Schlitz beer is pure. It offered details as to *why* the beer is pure. There may have been other beer companies that used the exact same process — but they didn't tell the story in their advertising.

This Claude Hopkins story illustrates to my clients *why* I want to learn details about their business that an average marketing expert or *ad man* may not ask for. Sometimes details can be shared in marketing that will only be revealed through a full immersion into a business. There may be things in operations that will help me determine a better marketing angle.

This story that I use from Schlitz has more impact than simply telling the client, "I need to know all about your business because it may give me ideas I may not have thought about."

The marketplace is a marketing battleground

Your competitors are snipers who try to pick your customers off. The government, regulatory agencies, DVRs, Do-Not-Call lists, the end of broadcast fax, SPAM filters, and more — make it harder for you to market to potential customers. Businesses completely outside of your category compete for your customers' attention, time, and money. The best tactic to cut through advertising clutter and to get your customers' attention, and build emotional attachment and loyalty to your business — is to *tell stories*. Stories are interesting. They get and keep attention.

Your competitors can copy your operations, your marketing style, and your marketing media, but they cannot copy your story. It is unique to you. Instead of only telling your story, gather stories to share with your customers about other customers, employees, as well as stories to illustrate the point that your business, service, or product is the obvious best choice.

Stories can be used business-to-business in the same way that I use the Schlitz story. Businesses that sell to consumers are wise to share stories that humanize the business. Put a picture in your customers' minds that your business is simply a group of humans working together with an owner who is a human being who has human issues just like the customer. Create the idea in their minds that you are not just a corporate logo or jingle.

Much of the marketing on the battleground is boring. A snoozer. Use stories to make your marketing *and* your organization interesting. Otherwise yours is just another boring ad for your potential customer to avoid.

As we wrap up this chapter, I will tell you a true story that is hard to believe

My wife and I celebrated our wedding anniversary about six weeks after my heart attack. To celebrate over the years, we've gone to beaches and mountain areas for relaxation and fresh air. This year my wife had a different idea. Jean said, "Let's go to a St. Louis Cardinals game for our anniversary."

I have been a Cardinals fan for over 30 years; my wife married into it. Although this sounded like an awesome anniversary idea, I was hesitant because it had only been three weeks since my heart attack. I was unsure about travelling. But my wife harped about it because she wanted to do something special for me after the traumatic event. I finally agreed to look at the Cardinals' schedule to see if they were even in town near our anniversary. I secretly thought — and hoped — that they could be on a 10-game road trip and I wouldn't have to admit that I was nervous about flying — even if it meant that I would miss going to a Cardinals game.

I pulled up the Cardinals schedule and wouldn't you know it, the Cardinals had a home game against the Pirates on the exact date of our anniversary. I clicked on the date thinking there might not be any tickets left. Not only were tickets available, it was Christian Day at Busch Stadium. The managers from both teams, Clint Hurdle and Mike Matheny, as well as star players such as Adam Wainwright and Matt Holliday were scheduled to speak after the game. Well, this news voided any previous attempt by me to get out of travelling on our anniversary. For my wife and me, Christian Day in St. Louis was something we would not miss.

St. Louis suffered a heat wave a few days prior to our arrival. Conditions were around 113 degrees and humid. Ironically, on Christian Day some people complained that it was "hot as hell." The star Cardinals pitcher that day, Adam Wainwright, got rocked. It was one of the worst outings of his career. This made for good fodder later, as Adam explained at the post-game gathering, "Sometimes you have good days and sometimes you have days like I had today — but God is always good."

A few months later I looked through the *J. Peterman* catalog. It contains examples of the best story-telling tactics to sell merchandise. So much so, I often read it for entertainment. If the name J. Peterman sounds familiar it is because it was the name of Elaine's boss in Seinfeld. The character played by John O'Hurley was an eccentric businessman and world traveler. The character in the show was based on the actual John Peterman and his catalog. The J. Peterman Company was around before the show. If you are a Seinfeld fan, you probably remember Mr. Peterman's deep, velvety voice and style he used to describe everything — in a detailed, interesting story. The ads are written in the same style. If you get the catalog you will hear his voice in your head while you read the ads.

In the catalog I found the most unique cufflinks I had ever seen. They were silver and the face was made out of the fabric of a Major League game-used baseball. At the time there were three teams to choose from. You could pick a team and the cufflinks would be made from a ball that was used during one of that team's games sometime during that year. You didn't get to pick a specific game, but you got to choose one of three teams. One of those teams was the St. Louis Cardinals. My wife looked over my shoulder and saw the cufflinks while I considered buying them. She jumped in, "You have to get those cufflinks. Imagine the conversation starter that would be."

Little did I know the true story I could tell later in any conversation.

So I purchased the cufflinks. When they arrived I couldn't wait to open the box. They were everything I thought they would be and more — much more. Stamped on the back of the cufflinks was something I didn't expect. There was an eight digit number. Included in the box was a card explaining that a game-used ball was used to make the cufflinks. The card also explained how Major League Baseball had launched the first league-wide authentication program in professional sports in 2001. It stated that the stamp with the ID number guarantees authenticity. The note instructed me to enter the eight digit authentication code into mlb.com/authentication to discover the specific game that the ball came from.

Unbelievably, my cufflinks were made from a ball used on our anniversary on Christian Day — the same game that my wife and I attended!

CHAPTER 2

Stealth Marketing

D evelopment for aircraft stealth technology began before World War I.

RADAR (Radio Detection and Ranging) had not been invented, so detection by visibility was the sole concern. In other words, the military's goal was to create invisible aircraft. In 1912, German designers produced a nearly invisible airplane. Its wings and fuselage were covered by a transparent material derived from cellulose, commonly used as the basis of movie film. To further reduce visibility, interior struts and other parts were painted with light colors. When flown at 900 feet, the plane was effectively invisible from the ground.[8]

RADAR was finally invented during World War II. As a result, defense focus shifted from creating invisible aircraft toward being undetectable to the enemy's high-tech anti-aircraft countermeasures. Hence, the invention of RADAR-stealthy technology.

In the same way, your marketing should be invisible to your competitors but highly visible to your customers/clients/patients. In addition, your marketing should go undetected to anti-advertising countermeasures such as DVRs, SPAM filters, Do-Not-Call lists, Opt-Out Yellow Pages, Banner blindness, ad-blockers, *no soliciting* signs, and short attention spans.

Direct Mail is stealth marketing to thwart anti-marketing countermeasures

The day after my heart attack I was supposed to go to Dan Kennedy's Mailbox Millions workshop. My plane ticket was purchased, my hotel in Cleveland booked, and I had my ticket to get into his high-level event. In my opinion, Kennedy is one of the industry's top direct mail experts and copywriters on planet Earth. His workshop consisted of three days of advanced training about how to use direct mail to market and grow your business. (In an aside, I find it incredible that some people think direct mailing is as simple as licking a stamp and sending their offer. Wrong!)

I was still in the hospital, so I missed Kennedy's workshop. Fortunately I have already used direct mail in creative ways for my company and for clients; I have studied the effectiveness of direct mail and it works — just as Kennedy teaches.

Direct mail — my first love and secret weapon

David Ogilvy, owner of Ogilvy and Mather which was one of the largest advertising agencies in the world during its heyday, said this in his book, *Ogilvy on Advertising*, "I do not regard advertising as entertainment or an art form, but as a medium of information. When I write an advertisement, I don't want you to tell me that you find it 'creative.' I want you to find it so interesting that you *buy the product*."

If you are sincerely interested in having people buy your service or product, consider how Ogilvy feels about direct mail. In *Ogilvy on Advertising*, Chapter 12 is titled, *Direct mail, my first love and secret weapon*.

Is that a bird flying around our office?

Ogilvy was hired to create and launch a marketing campaign to sell $750,000 Cessna executive jets. Cessna officials wanted him to use a theme that was related to aviation or flight.

Here is what Ogilvy did: Mysterious cartons were delivered to the offices of select CEOs. When they opened the carton, they found a live homing pigeon with a memo tied to its leg. On the memo was a place for the CEOs to put their names and addresses. The memo also read, *"If you would like a test flight in a Cessna Citation jet, release me."* Many of the prospective plane buyers wrote their information as instructed on the note and released the pigeons to fly home.

Look at the following statistics from the Cessna aerial assault:

- 800 prospects — executives of New York companies

- $15,000 marketing cost
- 114 pigeons returned to Ogilvy with response forms filled out
- Sold four jets — at $1 million each

If you can't bear the thought of using pigeons, or if the $15,000 investment doesn't pencil out for selling your service or product, you can use a plethora of other creative methods. Pigeon carriers may not work for you; neither will slapping a stamp on an envelope and sending a basic message to any ol' prospect.

You must put strategic thought and planning into your direct mail campaign just like you do with anything else that affects your business.

In search of magical whiz-bang technology

Successful business owners don't chase after shiny objects like a kitten would. Because the thought of using direct mail may seem old and antiquated to some, and because there is a lack of understanding about the true power of direct mail, I will address common questions:

Q: Why use direct mail when email is free?

A: Email is not free. It requires less monetary investment, but it certainly isn't free on your schedule. Using it requires your time and your prospect's time. Email open rates are lower than effective direct mail open rates. Ogilvy's pigeons probably earned 100 percent open-rates. Granted, the homing-pigeon campaign provided an advantage because it was highly unusual. However, using effective direct mail strategies can earn open rates and response rates that dwarf email results. When someone checks their email they are a button click away from distractions such as social media or another more enticing email — and the delete button.

I use a knife to cut meat and a spoon to eat soup. Both work for their task. If you were to invite me to your favorite restaurant for a working lunch during a consulting day and I ordered soup and a piece of chicken, I suspect the waiter would give me a spoon, a knife, and a fork. It does not have to be either/or. Use email marketing *and* direct mail. Your cost per *opened* email message will be significantly less than direct mail. Figure out a way to measure the effectiveness of both — calculate ROI and promote accordingly.

Q: Why use direct mail when we have this thing called the Internet?

A: It is true that there are things you can do on the Internet that you can't do in direct mail. One example is presenting a video sales letter that encourages prospects to fill out an interest form to be delivered to you — the business owner — within seconds. There are a number of other examples, but remember that marketing does not have to be either/or. Information and advertising delivered via direct mail is considered more trustworthy than most media. That fact is addressed later in this chapter. A common successful strategy uses direct mail to drive people to your website.

Q: Why use direct mail when I can mingle and interact with people using social media?

A: Social media is called *social* media for a reason. It's *social*. If you want to connect with old friends using social media and look at their cutesy baby pictures and funny dog videos — enjoy. It is true that social media works better for some industries than it does for others. Your definition of what social media is used for could be different than mine.

When I think of social media as a business tool, I think about trying to engage your customers in public conversation. Most customers probably don't want to converse with you publicly nearly as much as they want to look at pics of dogs, cats, and babies while commenting on their friends' new outfits, talking about their favorite baseball team, or debating about politics. They don't know you on a personal level.

Social media can be a big time-suck as you try to figure out how to get anyone to pay attention to you.

Direct mail holds attention better than social media. Printed newsletters sent via postal mail is a comparable *content sharing* media. The goal of both is to engage your customer, grow your relationship with your customer, and generate referrals. Social media may provide more immediate feedback, but actual time spent with your content that is sent by direct mail is much higher. That will become evident in coming chapters.

Clickable ads such as pay-per-click or pay-per-impression on social media platforms are not part of the comparisons that I just listed. These are direct response advertising rather than social media by definition.

Q: Why use direct mail when I can launch a Google Adwords Pay-Per-Click (PPC) Search campaign and reach millions by tomorrow?

A: I have launched, managed, and analyzed Google PPC campaigns for clients and non-clients who spend anywhere from $3,000 per month to over $1 million per year. I am a fan of using Google PPC *Search* for a host of industries, but it is primarily an inbound marketing media. This means that you only reach people who have come searching for

what you offer. That is a good strategy and one I often recommend. However, what about potential customers who
have not considered a new "widget" or whatever it is that
you sell? There are people who may need to be reminded
about your service or introduced to it for the first time because they won't know about it otherwise.

Keep in mind that your Google Ads are also alongside all
of your competitors and a button click away from a number
of distractions. However, your direct mail piece is probably
in the mailbox all by its lonesome; it almost certainly is not
alongside seven other competitors who have a Google PPC
ad too.

You can run Google Display ads and put your offer in
front of people who are not yet looking for it, just like direct
mail does. This can also work well. I recommend using it —
to an extent. Keep in mind that Google Display ad targeting
is not as precise as direct mail.

All of the media and strategies I just covered in the Q
& A can be used effectively under the right circumstances.
When comparing one media versus another, it is imperative
to realize that there is no single reason to use just one media or strategy. Come up with tweaks, new messaging, and
new targeting to get a variety of media to work for you. Pile
strategy on top of strategy.

Use one media to support another. For example, use direct mail to drive potential customers online where your
message takes on a different form — instead of text there is
a video. Now you have *touched* your customer by using two
different forms of media. When you generate a return using
different media sources, you build a fortified position. This

leaves your competition scratching their heads and thinking, *Why are you so much more successful than me?*

Fast facts about advertising principles:

Your advertising has to be seen to work

A special report from SIFO Research International regarding *Advertising Avoidance* shows that "everyone"
avoids something and 22 percent avoid everything. When
we study the distribution of avoiders within various media
categories, we can see that as many as 22 percent state that
they actively avoid advertising in all six media channels.[9]

People pay good money to **avoid** advertising by using
DVRs. Yet three in five American consumers report that
they enjoy getting postal mail from certain brands about
new products. The preference for receiving direct mail marketing was considerably higher than email which was 43
percent. The preference for direct mail extends to the 18
to 34-year-old demographic in both the U.S. and Canada[10]

You have to get their attention and interest for your marketing to work

Fifty-nine percent of U.S. respondents and 65 percent of
Canadian respondents agreed with the following statement,
"I enjoy getting postal mail from brands about new prod-
ucts."[11]

Trust is critical if you want people to buy from you

The media you use matters. Twenty-six percent of consumers rank direct mail as more trustworthy than email.
Direct mail was ranked as three times more trustworthy
than social media and blogs.[12]

For maximum results, your marketing should be memorable

One neuro-science case study revealed: The work conducted on this project — to study the brain's reaction to different forms of media — went to a level not seen before in market research. Tangible materials leave a deeper footprint in the brain. It is better connected to memory because it engages with its spatial memory networks.[13]

If you want your message to be in front of your prospects right away, use direct mail

Ninety-eight percent of consumers retrieve their mail from the mailbox the day it's delivered, with 77 percent sorting through it that same day.[14]

Examples of media use — good and bad:

Political ads are wily

If you want to experience a powerful example of an organization that successfully uses direct mail, make a donation to the political national committee of your choice. You will get emails and phone calls, but the postal mail will be eye-opening. Most of the time it will consist of paper inside of an envelope. The outside of the envelope will have teaser copy. Inside, you will find a conversational and compelling message — a call-to-action with persuasive copy written by some of the highest paid copywriters in the world. Don't give it to your English teacher, though. She would probably give it an "F" due to improper grammar, commas in wrong places, incorrect paragraph spacing and the like. There is a reason for this — to maintain readership. They don't care about getting an "A" from a school teacher. However, if you make a donation to a political national committee, you will become a student again as you witness copywriting masters demonstrate how to accomplish a goal by effectively using direct mail and copywriting.

Get more than your foot in the door

Because I live in hot Henderson, Nevada, before summer starts I get 15 to 20 postcards from air conditioning companies that all look about the same. The copy is full of special prices and discounts.

Marketing by price is a losing proposition. Most businesses offer similar discounts but no other differentiating criteria. So I go to Google and read their online reviews.

If you don't give your customer a differentiator, they will find one. I give credit to the AC guys who do the "$25 AC inspection," then use fear-based terminology to get in your door. They give the worst case scenario of losing your AC when it is 100 degrees outside. It happened to me once. By selling the inspection, the AC company gets their foot in the door and begins a relationship.

A rainy climate equivalent would be roofing companies that offer to clean your home's gutters. It is a way to get in the door so that when you need a $20,000 roof replacement, they are first on your list. Neither the gutter cleaning nor the $25 inspection is a money-maker for these companies. They are meant to generate leads so that when the big purchase is needed, they have an advantage over their competition. A chiropractor could offer $10 lunchtime neck massages just to get people in the door. There are a number of examples — all start with using direct mail to find interested parties.

Handouts bring the crowd

If you sell higher-ticket home improvement items such as air conditioners, marble countertops, flooring, roofing and the like, you can send out a 10x10 neighborhood mailer before, during, and after an installation.

With your new customer's permission, send a letter to 10 neighbors across the street and five neighbors on either side of your new installation. The first letter could say, "*We are going to be installing "X" at your neighbor's home next week. Stop by and say, "Hi!" You can take a look at "X" or take a sample home with an informational handout, business card, fast-action coupon, and a free consultation while we are in the area.*" A second letter tells the neighbors that you have arrived; "*Come by.*" The third letter would be, "*We're finished. Take a look at the completed product. Here is what your neighbor had to say about our service, team, and time commitments* (insert testimonial). *We can do the same for you.*" (Insert call-to-action).

Stand out from the rest

Local business owners who sell most of their products and services to a certain geographical area could tweak the 10x10 method to make it work. Real estate agents do a lesser version of this; they mail more than the 20 in my example. Unfortunately, the handouts usually inform that *Joe Smith just sold his home in your neighborhood. For a free estimate of your home's value, call XXX-XXXX.* Real estate agents could get a lot more leads by adding a testimonial from the homeowner to the piece of paper with some type of lower-threshold lead-generator. A lead-generator could be a free report such as, *How to Prepare Your Home To Earn the Maximum Sale Price.* Agents would also be wise to encourage neighbors to receive the agent's newsletter.

Google —$66 billion in 2014 from online advertising

They earned $66 billion from online advertising, yet — the head honchos at Google market the company's services to business owners via postcards and letters via direct mail. You may have received one with a $100 Adwords coupon. Direct mail is also used to promote Google's directory for local businesses. If you run an agency or are a consultant like myself, you may have received a slew of $100 Adwords coupons, training packets, and invitations to *expert* events in order to learn more about using Google Adwords for your clients.

Using multi-media effectively

I teach car dealers how to follow-up by using direct mail. Sometimes a prospective customer will fill out an inquiry form about a certain vehicle, or an online application. An automated email response is typically sent to the potential customer. Then a salesperson calls the promising prospect on the phone and doesn't get a response. So they email and call again; with still no response.

I teach my clients to send personalized letters via postal mail. Some people don't want to talk on the phone for the same reason that they don't come to the place of business — because it is uncomfortable for them for whatever reason. They don't want to be pressured. They don't want to be bombarded with emails, so they think that by not responding you will leave them alone. Sending a personalized letter in the mail gets you behind enemy lines. This is not to suggest that your customer is the enemy — the true enemy is perceptions fueled by others who will cause your prospect to avoid you.

There are limits

Most media has limited reach. If you are reliant on SEO and PPC, you are subject to the number of people who are searching. If Facebook users top 200 million in America alone, that leaves over 100 million Americans who are not on Facebook. But I'll bet that those 100 million probably have an old-fashioned mailbox.

If you offer a service or product that you sell B2B, direct mail may be the only way to reach your prospective client. Not as many business owners and decision-makers mingle on Facebook where they might be exposed to your advertisement. Their gate-keepers answer the phone. And it's true that their gatekeepers intercept their postal mail on some occasions. But I know about some sneaky, ethical, and entertaining tricks to get past the postal mail gatekeeper.

Don't be annoying

Some types of media are considered a nuisance. Too much email is annoying. Speak with anyone and you will hear the same complaint, "I get too many emails." Phone calls at any time are mostly unwelcome.

Not too long ago, I received *three* phone calls in one week from one of the largest insurance companies in the world. The first time, I was fairly short with the caller and I told them that I was happy with the insurance I already had. The *cold call specialist* was persistent, which I don't normally mind, but I was busy. During the second call I was brusque. I reminded the person that I had already received a phone call from someone else within their organization. "Please stop calling me," I said. During the third call I hardly let the person speak. My irritation was evident in my tone as I said, "This is the third call. I am NOT interested. Do NOT call me again."

The funny thing is, because of my career choice I purposely watch commercials, purchase stuff and behave in a way that I know will put myself in front of advertisements. I subscribe to online lists and request to receive advertising. However, phone calls *never* come at a good time. Spam emails are *always* aggravating. Plenty of advertising interrupts you when you are in the middle of doing something else. Interruptions break your concentration, infiltrate your private space, and even disrupt your relaxation time. Direct mail is always *at your convenience*.

Like others in the previously mentioned Epsilon study, I enjoy receiving direct mail. In fact, after a number of phone calls from a political committee I finally said, "Stop calling, send more direct mail." That was as blunt as I could be.

You've tried direct mail and it didn't work for you

When new clients invest in a consulting day or phone consultation with me, I request a peek at all the marketing and advertising they currently use and what they have used in the past. Many times I critique a direct mail campaign that didn't deliver desired results. Here are a few tips so that you can increase your chance of success with your next direct mail campaign:

Target

You can't sell steak to a vegetarian. A person's widely-held beliefs or strong loyalties to another brand are challenging to overcome. If they happen to come to your place of business on their own and want to purchase — by all means, sell. However, when investing money to acquire a new customer, pick the low-hanging fruit. Consider reasonable targets. I ask new car dealer clients in what radius can they realistically sell vehicles. The answer I often get is 100 miles, 50 miles. Unless you sell a unique brand such as Rolls Royce, don't expect to sell to a large geographical target. Do a better job of marketing to the more ideal target. Finer points regarding this approach will be discussed in another chapter.

Copywriting

Your message should influence. Make it clear why someone should buy from you. Your message should be unique. It is even more important to be unique if you are in an industry where trust is low. When setting up a new Google PPC campaign, I preview all of my client's competitors' advertisements by having my team put relevant keywords into Google. Those ads are then copied onto a Word document and printed out. I read through the ads to make sure our advertisements are different. In the stealth marketing known as direct mail, this is difficult to do, but you get the idea about the importance of having a unique message.

Split-test

To turn good results into great results, split-test your marketing list. When I critique an advertisement I can usually make recommendations for improvement from scratch. However, when possible it is always best to split-test.

A split-test is simply sending two versions of a similar advertisement to a comparable group of people. Measure responses and select a winner. Your winner is now *the control*. Mail the control to the rest of your list.

For example: John has a mailing list of 10,000 people. John is unsure if a 10 percent discount is favorable in comparison to a *gift-with-purchase*. So I write two versions of one similar sales letter for John. In version A there is a 10 percent discount offer. Version B offers a free Android Tablet with purchase. We mail version A to 2,500 people and version B to another 2,500 people. We find that version B earned a 3 percent response while version A earned a 1 percent response. As a result, we mail version B to the remaining 5,000 people.

At first glance you might think a 2 percent bump in response isn't a big deal. However, the actual measurement reveals a 200 percent improvement in response.

Lead generator

Your first priority is to make sales. However, there are a lot of people who are not ready to buy yet, no matter what you offer or say. The timing isn't right. They have to take the kids to camp. Their spouse is out of town. They just bought something else and the budget is thin. There are a number of reasons. They might be interested, just not right now at this moment.

The list of people who are interested but not yet ready to buy is a larger number than people who are ready to buy now — barring a perfectly-timed mailing. Don't let those future sales get away. Put in a hard-to-resist offer for someone who is not quite ready to buy. Get them to raise their hand by filling out a form on your website, calling a phone number, or return something to you via prepaid postage return mail.

Follow-up

Unless you sell spontaneously-purchased items such as candy bars positioned at the check-out line of the grocery store, you need follow-up. You *must* have follow-up for generated leads. Do not expect your potential customer to remember you. It is not their job to remember you. It is your job to remind them *why* they were interested a month ago. Follow-up to individual prospects is a challenge. In the next chapter, I share a simple solution to this dilemma.

Be interesting

A *New York Times* article from 1988 stated that the average number of advertisement and brand exposures per day per person is more than 5,000. The ad is titled, *Advertising; Ad Clutter: Even in Restrooms Now*. In my experience, as the article title suggests, I haven't come across a men's restroom without an advertisement above the urinal. My wife tells me it is the same in the ladies room.

You must stand out from the clutter. The postal mailbox is almost empty these days, so that is a start. But even then, your business needs to be interesting. Your marketing should offer value in and of itself. It should be interesting to read and to open. Conversational copy engages the reader. Interesting stories and pictures keep their attention and interest. Involvement devices and gadgets to get your direct mail recipient to interact with your correspondence are powerful — when used appropriately.

You, the Commander-in-Chief

To win a battle, the Commander-in-Chief doesn't order a lone strike. In the same vein, you shouldn't "one-and-done" your direct mail. Your direct mail campaign should be a continuous battle to get past countermeasures already in place. In the next chapter, you will find an effective method to increase your odds of being rewarded. As Commander-in-Chief, you need to know how to deploy stealth tactics to grow and protect your business.

CHAPTER 3

Department of Defense (DOD)

W hat good is having a military juggernaut if you can't protect the homeland?

Have you wondered why you lose customers? Are you tracking the following?

- Customers lost
- Customer drop-off point
- Repeat purchases
- Referrals per customer

If you track those four items, you will uncover hidden wealth in your business. From there, you can work to excavate every hidden asset in your business.

Each chapter in this book reveals ways to earn **new** business. This chapter will do the same while protecting the business you **already** have.

Acquisition cost of a new customer is amongst the highest of all expenses in your business. However, your existing customers are more likely to buy from you again. According to Marketing Metrics, your probability of selling to a new prospect is 5-20 percent, and your probability of selling to an existing customer is 60-70 percent. Existing customers are more likely to upgrade in the future or buy a premium option. They are more likely to send referrals. Existing customers are more forgiving when you make a mistake because they have experienced good service in the past. Your existing customers' perceptions about you are better than their opinions about your industry as a whole, which is only a starting point for potential new customers.

Some business owners mistakenly think that taking care of your customers and delivering on your promises leads to loyalty. That does contribute in a big way, but you need to do more for maximum success.

Remember that your customers are bombarded with non-stop messages to buy elsewhere. These messages are often written by experienced copywriters who make persuasive arguments for why your customer should buy from your competitor. These messages may come from your direct competitors who sell the same product or service. They may come from indirect competitors who sell an alternative to your offer. Or the competition may be completely unrelated to your business but your customer's pocket is emptied, leaving them with nothing left to purchase your offer.

Places where people see advertisements:

- Billboards while driving
- Television while driving — ridiculous and dangerous, but true
- Above urinals
- Urinal cakes — people really do advertise on something that men pee on. I wonder if women are subjected to all this creative bathroom advertising. Are there signs on the back of the stall door, "While you sit here..."
- Leaning back in dental chair — on the ceiling
- While getting gasoline, there are signs and videos that play just below the indicator gauge
- Direct mail is limitless and that makes all of your customers at risk — as pointed out in the last chapter
- Co-op direct mail that allows multiple businesses to split costs for printing and postage (you can do this too — revealed in a few pages)
- Text messages — a cell phone is the one thing that your customer has on them at all times
- While looking at friends' baby pictures on social media
- During a television show — in content advertising
- Before a movie — ads run prior to the start of each movie
- During the movie — product placement

- Other people's happy customers who work like volunteer soldiers and constantly refer business (you will discover this for your business in a later chapter)
- Magazines — print and online
- Newspapers — print and online
- Yellow Pages — print and online
- On the windshields of their vehicles after exiting a store
- Bus stop bench. Why do realtors advertise here? Do people who ride buses buy homes?
- Google Adwords — Search and Display
- Email ads
- Facebook ads
- YouTube ads
- In-store ads — new product or service similar to yours, or in-store ads for a strategic alliance partner in the same category as your business
- And the list goes on…

There are more types of advertising than what I've listed and new ways to advertise that will evolve. Maybe someday we will have a chip installed in our ears and businesses can bid on sending their ad straight into our brains. Better yet, it can be like the movie *Inception*; just plant the idea into our heads for a specified dollar amount.

But seriously, advertising is everywhere.

Have you wondered what form of media or advertisement was put in front of your *EX*-customer that led them astray?

If you could figure it out perhaps you could deploy a battalion to destroy it.

Until that day, protect your existing customers. In addition to great service, a variety of ways to do that include:

- Customer loyalty programs
- Membership programs
- Regular customer appreciation events
- Customer newsletters

Setting up Your Department of Defense

From the previous bulleted list, the method that warrants the most attention are Customer Newsletters.

Publication

Your printed newsletter is viewed by your customer as a publication, not advertising — especially if you send a printed version at regular intervals. A publication allows people to put down their anti-advertising defenses and consume your content. Your publication can contain a mix of advertising — sometimes blatant, sometimes not — and it should contain interesting content for the reader. Some of the examples that follow are magazines and for the companies using them, it makes sense. For others, a newsletter makes more sense and serves the same purpose.

Mix in products and services

In 2014, Costco was the second-largest retailer in the world with net revenues surpassing $110 billion. Costco achieved that with 464 stores compared to Walmart's 5,109 stores. Costco stores earn more than twice as much per location than Walmart, the largest retailer in the world.[15]

From 2009 to 2013 while competitors lost business to the Internet, Costco's sales grew 39 percent.[16]

Something relevant to this chapter that separates Costco from the other top 20 revenue-earning retailers is their monthly publication. *Costco Connection* is a magazine sent to Business and Executive members. It is the largest-circulation print monthly in the United States with 8.6 million subscribers. Ginnie Roeglin, the magazine's publisher for the last 16 years, said, "We see about 56 percent of our subscribers a month buy something at one of our stores based on something they've read in the magazine."[17]

Costco Connection contains articles about home improvement, celebrities, recipes and more, all wrapped around a slew of co-op advertisements and Costco merchandise coupon ads. Don't think the readers and subscribers are a bunch of lower-economic class coupon clippers, because a survey of 860 households with an annual income of $250,000 revealed that *Costco Connection* is the second most read magazine after *People* and just ahead of *National Geographic*.[18]

Humanize

A newsletter can transform you and your business from a nameless, faceless, personality-less company into a group of human beings who customers can relate to, trust, and refer to. Adding the human element makes your customers less likely to cross enemy lines and go to your competitors no matter how much advertising they are exposed to.

Although Lee Iacocca didn't do it through publication, the humanizing of Chrysler was part of his success. Alan Mulally did the same thing with Ford Motor Company.

Johnny Carson was wildly popular because he shared personal stories. Johnny wasn't shy about discussing his failed marriages and alimony payments. Offer personal stories in your newsletter to add the human element to endear your fans/clients/customers.

Be a part of something

When your customers receive your monthly newsletter containing entertainment, stories, and interactive pieces, they feel like they are part of something. You can deliver a newsletter to all of your customers or only pick a select portion. Either way, you want them to feel special. You may bring recognition to some of your customers in your newsletter, barring legal reasons or privacy issues, by singling them out with kudos for a variety of accomplishments.

Not many companies have customers who get tattoos of their company logo inked over all areas of their body. But Harley Davidson is one such company. In 1983, Harley officials tried to convince the public of their product's renewed credibility. They began an intense marketing campaign, *Super Ride Program*. Part of the campaign included starting Harley Owners Groups (H.O.G.) which came with a free one-year membership in a local riding group, along with other benefits. Members received a subscription to a bi-monthly publication that included H.O.G. tales packed with riding stories, product info, H.O.G. news, and member stories. H.O.G. registered 73,000 members that year. By 2014, with a circulation of more than 800,000, the magazine was widely considered one of the most valuable benefits of membership in the Harley Owners Group.[19] Marketing VP Kathleen Lowler-Demitors said, "It humanized the company and not only gave customers direct access to the Harley family, but it also allows them to feel like one of the family."[20]

Increase customer loyalty and repeat business

Your newsletter should have personality, fun, and entertainment value. This leads your customer to WANT to read it. It also builds the relationship you have with them and increases the familiarity and comfort level with you. Most likely that the only times that your customers currently hear from you is when you ask for their money.

Brand-building

If you have heard me speak at a convention or workshop, or if you have read my published articles in industry magazines, you know that I do not like to see companies waste money on brand advertising. Wasted branding happens when you promote your brand to people who will never buy from you. You should sell products and services to build a brand, not branding to sell products and services. Your existing customers care about your brand and are more likely to refer to it in a positive way when you focus on building your brand to THEM, and then let them build your brand to others. Your newsletter is an affordable, brand-building opportunity.

Top-of-mind

Quick - what did you eat for breakfast two days ago?

How many advertisements can you recall from yesterday? A primary purpose of brand-building is to stay top-of-mind when it is time for your customer to purchase in your product category. Your newsletter/monthly publication keeps you in front of your customers and top-of-mind, which will lead to referrals, new purchases, and upgrades.

Every month, your newsletter will have a reminder that referrals are welcome AND rewarded, if that is something you offer.

Staying power and pass-around value

Because your newsletter is viewed as a publication instead of an advertisement, it will stick around longer. Don't be surprised if one of your customers references content from a newsletter that they received three months ago. It likely sits on their coffee table and they thumbed through it again yesterday. Your customer may be done with your newsletter, but because it has value and is not to be thrown out with normal junk mail, they may leave it in the workplace break room — where others have a chance to see it. It may linger in the break room for weeks because no one wants to throw it away. Newsletters, magazines, and books all have this affect.

Fight off companies with bigger budgets

The best way to get your customers to cover their eyes to other advertising is to have a relationship with them. A newsletter with personality will strengthen relationships.

Fight off smaller companies

Smaller companies tend to have closer relationships with customers. This is an advantage. Smaller companies can use the "we treat our customers like family" message more effectively than larger companies. Launching a customer newsletter is a faster method to build intimate relationships with customers.

Avoid random acts of marketing

If you are in a business that requires custom responses to new leads, in specific situations you may not have the proper material to send. Keep a few extra copies of each month's newsletter on hand. It will give you something to send and it will make you stand out. You want to get something in your new lead's hand as soon as they show interest. If you are in an industry where customers contemplate for a long period of time before purchasing, a newsletter is more than just handy — it's a constant reminder to your lead as to why they showed interest in your business in the first place.

Build expert status

Being perceived as an expert is more important than most entrepreneurs realize. Everyone wants to work with *the* expert. It makes the customer feel like they are making or have made a good purchasing decision. Other than the poorest of individuals who have to purchase the cheapest no matter what, your customers will be more loyal to you and refer more business if they believe that you are the #1 expert. If they have faith that you are the expert, they will brag about you to their friends because it makes them feel good about themselves. A newsletter is something that experts publish. For most business owners, only book authorship surpasses a newsletter publication for achieving expert status. *Resource BookByInterview.com

Platform

A newsletter is one of the various types of platforms. Bill O'Reilly's television show is his platform. Every time he authors a new book and mentions it on his show, it is a bestseller almost immediately. I'll bet it is mostly his regular viewers who buy his books so quickly.

Jimmy Fallon used his own platform (his television show) to advertise to his customers (viewers). This led to a bestselling children's book, *Your Baby's First Word Will*

Be Dada. Jimmy Fallon isn't a typical writer and he hasn't been a Dada for very long. Is he an expert on the subject? Not likely. However, he has a platform that he controls. He mentioned the release of his book using his platform and BAM — bestseller.

Psychologist Phil McGraw used someone else's platform to achieve great success. He appeared on *The Oprah Winfrey Show* in 1998. In 2002, McGraw launched his own syndicated daytime talk show, *Dr. Phil*. McGraw is the author of six #1 *New York Times* bestsellers. After using Oprah's platform to grow his fame, Dr. Phil used his own platform to launch best-selling books.

They are all platforms

Many examples I've referenced here are people who were made famous on television which lead to increased financial wealth. My point is that it all happened because of a platform. Your newsletter is a platform where you will create stronger relationships, launch new products and services of your own, or co-op with someone else.

Jay Abraham, business executive, conference speaker, and best-selling author, utilized other people's newsletters as a platform to make millions of dollars for at least one of his business ventures.

A regularly scheduled newsletter can attract co-op, cross-promotion, and strategic alliance partners which will help you grow your business, benefit from the growth of their business, or help pay for the investment that you put into your newsletter platform.

For a checklist of things to put in your newsletter go to **KennyTalks.com**

CHAPTER 4

The United Nations

Shortly after Pearl Harbor was bombed by Japanese forces on December 7, 1941, President Franklin Roosevelt, British Prime Minister Winston Churchill, and Roosevelt aide Harry Hopkins drafted the "Declaration by United Nations" during a December 29 meeting at the White House.[21]

Shortly after that conference, The United States, United Kingdom, Soviet Union, France, China, and others formed The Allies of World War II in an official January 1, 1942 declaration.

After the end of World War II in 1945, countries who had fought in alliance against German, Japanese and Italian aggression banded together to form a stronger union and prevent such a conflict from ever happening again. The

United Nations (UN) was officially established on October 24, 1945. The second "war to end all wars" had lasted from 1939-1945.

Together, these countries had opposed the Axis powers and brought an end to the battle. The formal establishment of the UN set objectives to maintain worldwide peace and security, promote human rights, foster social and economic development, protect the environment, and provide humanitarian aid in cases of famine, natural disaster, and armed conflict.[22]

The United Nations is one of many strategic alliances formed by various countries with the goal of mutual benefit.

As a business owner, you should form strategic alliances for mutual benefit with other organizations and powerful people.

Starbucks struggled financially in the late 1980s. A failed attempt to expand into the Midwest and Canada was nearly disastrous. A few years later, Starbucks rebounded, due in large part to a series of strategic partnerships and alliances.

- In 1993, Starbucks partnered with Barnes and Noble bookstores to provide in-house coffee shops, benefiting both retailers.

- In 2006, Starbucks partnered with Apple iTunes to collaborate on selling music as part of the "coffee house" experience.[23]

By 2001, Starbucks had grown into an enterprise with more than 5,000 stores spread across four continents. Despite the recession, the company had opened a record number of stores, had posted their highest net earnings that year, and was named the fastest-growing global brand by *Business Week*.

Starbucks' management achieved stellar success without an extensive advertising and promotions budget. Over a 20-year period, Starbucks spent an average of about $1 million each year. For contrast, management for Proctor & Gamble's Pampers brand spend $30 million *per year* on advertising.[24]

Why you?

The long but not exhaustive list of various advertising methods from the previous chapter has saturated the market. This inundation makes it hard to get your prospective customers' attention.

With global news about major corporations and organizations' evil deeds, and distrust generated worldwide, it is difficult to gain the confidence of your potential customer. Major corporations that cook their books, pyramid schemes by major investors, vehicle recalls in the millions — all lead to consumer cynicism.

Add into the bad-news-mix that your customers' minds are full of their experiences with companies that have burned them with false promises, poor service, and self-serving sales. That is not your fault, but you have to deal with it.

If every person calculated all of their purchases ever made, they would realize the vast majority were with honest people. But the media doesn't report about honest organizations. It is not "selling" news to say that, *"JoJo's gave great customer service experience today."*

Customers find it easier to recall bad experiences over good experiences. It's easy these days for them to complain publicly — evidenced by the fact that it is challenging to get only one of your happy customers to write a positive online review. However, it is so easy to get them to write a negative online review — simply do something that makes them upset.

There are also a number of anti-advertising counter-measures that make it harder to reach your potential customer, such as: DVRs, SPAM filters, Do-Not-Call lists, Opt-Out Yellow Pages, Banner blindness, ad-blockers, no soliciting signs, and short attention spans.

So many different things compete to garner your prospective customers' attention, such as their mobile phone with 10 million apps and games. Notifications interrupt their focus when their phone buzzes with updates from Facebook, Twitter, Snapchat, Instagram, and Pinterest.

You must form an alliance to defeat a common enemy. Your foe may be a competitor, a new government regulation, or an unfair perception.

Benefits to having one or more alliance partnerships include sharing resources, expenses, and even risk. Divvy up products, distribution networks, manufacturing know-how, project funding, capital equipment, information, skills, and even intellectual property. Think of your partnerships as relationships which aim for cooperation; each partner's goal is to gain better benefits together than can be reached individually.

The best new customer

If the best new customer is a referral from an existing happy customer, then the second best is a referral from a strategic alliance partner. A Nielson study revealed that the number one most trusted form of advertising is, *"recommendations from people I know."*[25]

Recommendations from people I know can be a happy customer (discussed in a later chapter). It can also be people from a place of business that has already earned their trust and attention — who then refers a customer to your business.

When someone from another organization or business refers a customer to you, you benefit from *trust transference*. This speeds up the buying process. It also means the referred customer has conducted less or no research. That leads to less price resistance. *Trust transference* customers are more forgiving if their first experience isn't perfect. They think, *"Well, Joe from JoJo's Dry Cleaners referred me here. Maybe it was a one-time mistake."* People will pay more for trust. At every level of the economic ladder, people want to trust whom they do business with. The most important question in the minds of voters in a presidential election is, *"Is this person trustworthy?"*

Geography

One country partners with another for geographical reasons. If a country in the West has a problem with a country in the Middle East, the Western country partners with a different Middle-Eastern country to utilize their geographical location. Western troops build a base within their ally's country for strategic geographical advantages.

In the same way, you can partner with other businesses that have a geographical advantage. If you are in the western portion of a city and can't seem to sell to people located on the east side of the city due to distance and traffic, a partnership may work.

Marketing and advertising to the eastern portion of the city may not be profitable because you have to pay upfront for marketing. Your ROI on advertising to the eastern portion of the city may not be high enough to warrant your investment. Adding a location may not be profitable either.

Rather than give up on that area, partner with another business and refer business back and forth. If it doesn't make sense to refer business to them but they are willing to refer business to you, entice the company with a percentage of your profits. If the opportunity is big enough you may build a base. Think of it as your own embassy within another company's location such as Starbucks inside of Barnes and Noble.

Assets

Another company may have a larger sales force. It may not make sense for you to build a large sales team. The ramp-up time to build one is time that you could spend reaping profits if your larger team was already in place.

A western country may partner with a Middle-Eastern country by using a different military branch. The United States has strong military all the way around, but when battling in the Middle East, it may make sense to deploy ground troops. Military ground forces are strong but the terrain is foreign and may require partnering with another country's military branch who knows the terrain.

Similarly, another company may allow you to use their ground troops to grow your business. If the partnering company has a sales force that has free time during a portion of the day, you can spend that extra time selling your products and services. Or, your alliance partner's sales force may sell your product and service at the same time that they sell their own product and service.

Complementary

Military forces from different countries often work together to fight a common enemy. Their troops are complementary because they form a synergistic partnership. Your products and services may fit perfectly with another business that serves similar customers.

Your common enemy is everything that makes it harder to sell your products and services, such as regulations, unfair perceptions, and a competitor. A car dealership without its own repair shop can partner with an independent repair shop. When a dealer's vehicle needs to be repaired it is sent to only one repair shop. In turn, this repair shop's sales force sends its customers who need another vehicle to their partner dealership.

Another automotive alliance could be between an auto detail business and a repair shop. A dealership, auto detail business, and a repair shop can form an alliance to sell their services to the other two business's customers.

A chiropractor, masseuse, and acupuncturist can form a United Nations of their own by fighting a common enemy — back pain. If those services are too similar and siphon business from each other, any of them could partner with a golf course to market to golfers with back pain.

Expertise

Your company may have expertise to offer a non-competing business and/or their customers. Another company may have the ability to do the same for you.

For example, a convention planner asked me to speak at their event but they didn't quite have the budget. Instead, they paid a partial speaking fee and gave me a significant amount of free advertising in their publication that went out to their members. The convention planner exchanged resources (media) for my expertise for their members.

An interesting example:

Another highly profitable company asked to partner with us because they knew we could help their clients be more successful. They liked the idea that when their clients are more successful, those clients need more of their products and services. Everyone wins!

Media co-op

If a particular media makes sense to you but the investment prices you out of using it, you could partner with another company to split the cost. Real estate agents and mortgage lenders have done this for years. When you need one service, you automatically need the other so it makes sense that a real estate agent and a mortgage lender will advertise together. Direct mail is often used for this purpose. If you don't have time to find another company to partner with, consider a company such as Valpak which exists for this purpose. Valpak bunches several businesses into one package that is sent to consumers' homes.

Capital

Media co-op is used to save money on one particular method that would not be profitable any other way. If you are entirely new to a market, your upfront media expense may be through the roof. If you have no existing customers, capital flies out the door before you have a single one as you build your customer base. By approaching other organizations and businesses that already have access to your potential patron, you can move customer acquisition cost to after the sale. You will still pay to acquire a customer, but now you can grow the business.

Exchange of value

You scratch my back I scratch yours — or you scratch my customer's back and I scratch your customer's back. You may have value to offer another business whose managers do not want to create, build, or grow, and visa-versa. If another non-competing business can benefit your customers, why would you deprive your customers of its value? Use that same explanation to other businesses when you approach them about taking care of their customers. Put together a package with a letter to explain how you can offer their customers non-competing value.

If you are hesitant, or a potential alliance partner is hesitant

You or another business may be tentative about allowing access to your customers or clients. This feeling is typically due to one of three reasons:

1 - Don't understand the value — If someone whom you want to partner with doesn't understand the value of strategic alliances, give them a copy of this book.

2 - Don't want to allow access to someone who may take advantage of customers — This hesitancy is the most understandable. You should protect your customers just as another company wants to protect theirs. Running a business should not only be about the quick injection of money. Trust is first and foremost.

I suggest that you conduct live communication with the leadership of the company that you want to ally yours with and get to know them on a personal level. Research the other company as if you were going to refer your grandmother to purchase there.

3 - Feel uncomfortable about selling access to customers as if there is something wrong with that idea — Imagine that your clients are stranded on an island. There is no access to drinking water or food. Your product is bottled water and you happily provide it to them for a reasonable fee. They are happy and you are happy. Across the shark-infested waters from this island is another island where a farmer lives who has fresh food. You like your clients and have the ability, so you build a bridge. Your clients are thrilled with you. They now have access to food in addition to your water.

After the bridge is built, you open a toll booth to use it but you don't charge your clients. Instead, you charge the farmer on the other island to get across the bridge. As the toll booth operator, you make money, your clients get the food they need, and the farmer is happy too.

"The things we are rewarded for in business are the complex and consistent problems we solve for others, or the quality of

opportunities we make possible for others." ~Jay Abraham, business executive, conference speaker, author, and expert on Strategic Alliances

By building a bridge rather than trying to sell more water, you allowed your clients access to something they desperately needed (food) and increased your profits — while taking on zero risk.

In this story, it cost money and involved some financial risk to build a bridge. But there is a way to build a symbolic bridge without financial risk. Read on...

You already have a list of clients who need your help. They buy your products and services. You may solve a majority of your clients' needs, but you are probably not 100 percent of the solution toward what they need to reach their full potential. So sell your bread and butter but let someone else offer them jelly and jam...and you get a percentage of the profits. Or, using the bridge example, allow another service provider to cross your bridge and pay your toll along the way.

I am **not** suggesting you sell your customer list outright.

But if there is someone you trust that you believe could benefit your clients, why not allow that person to cross your bridge? It helps your customers and helps you.

The convention bridge

When you go to a trade show or a convention, planners are the toll booth that vendors pay in order to cross the bridge. Their attendees (customers) may pay a lesser toll to attend.

Convention hosts have massive lists of customers. They spend tens of thousands and even millions of dollars to market and invite them to conventions. They charge vendors to support the convention and to add value for attendees. They hire content speakers to attract certain groups of attendees and to provide value to all. Convention hosts make money by building their bridges. Attendees (their customers) benefit by receiving good content AND by exposure to a variety of vendors and their services. Everyone wins.

I have participated in all three sides of the previous convention example; I speak at them and offer value to attendees and vendors. The interesting thing that I have realized is that everyone involved contributes to the bridge.

- The convention owner builds the bridge
- The convention planner hires speakers to make the bridge better and attract more people to cross the bridge and pay a toll to cross the bridge
- Attendees pay a small toll to cross the bridge
- Vendors pay a larger toll to cross the bridge

Virtual convention bridge leverage

You and your existing clients can benefit with your own convention bridge — but you do not have to spend tens of thousands of dollars. In fact, you do not have to spend a penny.

One obvious benefit to you is that you earn profits with no loss or risk. But there are more, including:

- Your clients will appreciate your effort for the connection that helps their business grow.

- Your clients who do not take advantage of the connection will still appreciate your interest in their success even when it is not your product or service.

- You may boost your client's activity and create more need for your own product/service.

- You give yourself an economic and strategic advantage over your competitors by increasing your client's average value. This allows you to invest more into customer service or acquiring new clients.

- Re-engage clients who have slowed buying or communication with you; offer a better solution or an outside solution.

There is more to that last bullet point than meets the eye. Your profits will increase directly by letting someone else sell services to your clients and sharing in the profits.

You can take these profits and:

- Boost your customer service and strengthen existing relationships with existing clients.

- Acquire more customers using the same methods currently in use.

- Acquire more customers using methods that were *previously unaffordable*. This strategy gives you an economic advantage that your competitors probably do not have. You can spend more to acquire a customer. Your competitor can try to copy you and spend themselves broke — or give up and let you keep the #1 spot.

- Upgrade your existing office, equipment, software, etc.

- Use profits for sales training or marketing coaching to maximize your efforts.

- Go on vacation, buy another vehicle, home improvements, kids college fund, etc.

Whatever option you choose — you can stop working harder for your business and get your business to work harder for you.

Go to **KennyTalks.com** for a checklist of items to form strategic alliances. This resource includes methods to introduce a strategic alliance partner to an existing customer/client base.

CHAPTER 5

Soldiers

No military force can win a battle by using only drones.

High-tech equipment offers an advantage in battle, but you still need soldiers to operate equipment. You will also need ground troops.

Good marketing + good product/service + bad employees = decreased sales.

On the other hand, good marketing + good product/service + great employees = multiplied profits.

Starting today, pay close attention and observe what employees do in all of the places you frequent. Watch while they completely deviate from their training and instruction about how to give proper service. I've heard of and witnessed horrifying stories; some are worse than others. Before clients invest additional money in marketing, I may ask them to beef up their service and staff.

I have been on the receiving end of some customer service stories that you need to know about, not only for the entertainment factor, but to look introspectively at what goes on inside your business. Although you may be able to figure out which companies I refer to, names with an asterisk have been changed because of the awful behavior. I don't want to muddy the waters for these companies because they may be great, but the situation that I found myself in wasn't good.

Caveman Office Supply* — buying paper

After a consultation lunch and on the way back to my office, I got a call and learned that we were out of printer paper. We usually order in bulk and have it shipped. But we can't run out of paper, so I stopped at Caveman Office Supply.

Who knew there were so many choices of paper? I finally found what I thought was right and picked up a case that contained 3,000 pieces in six reams all in one box. *That should hold us over until our shipment comes in,* I thought.

On my way up to the counter I ran into an employee who wasn't texting or talking to another employee about last night's football game. I told him that all I needed was laser paper, but didn't see the right weight so I grabbed the all-purpose paper instead. The employee said that there was a laser specific option that was better. He took the big case out of my hands, put it back where I had picked it up, then handed me one ream of the correct paper. I appreciated his effort in carrying the box back for me and for finding the type of paper that I needed. But after I checked out I thought, *I hope this is enough to last me until my shipment arrives.* On the way out I walked past another paper aisle and saw a case of the same paper that the employee had handed to me — in one box with 3,000 pieces of paper in six reams. I was in a hurry and didn't have time to return the ream and purchase the case.

Although the employee was friendly and helpful in one way, he took money out of the owner's pocket (as I will explain in a few paragraphs.)

Wonky Auto Parts*

After church one Sunday, my wife and I got into our car, looking forward to a relaxing afternoon at home. I stuck the key into the ignition and twisted it...click, click, click, click. It would not start. The battery was dead. After attending the first service and helping with the five-year-old kids class for the second service, I was tired. Twenty-one five-year-olds wore me out.

Thankfully, there were plenty of nice people milling around in the parking lot and several people asked, "Need a jump?" After starting the car, I drove to a parts store on the way home to get the battery tested and replaced if needed. The employee was nice and helpful. He brought out a battery tester and determined that the battery was indeed dead. I said, "Fine, bring me a new one and hook it up." Being the nice guy that he was, it appeared that he wanted to look out for me because he told me that I could go, "Just down the road and save $10 at Walmart for the same battery." Well, I chose to buy the battery this company offered and have it installed right there on the spot. There is nothing wrong with Walmart, but I wanted the convenience and I wanted the service done right then. My wife and I were tired, hungry and hot.

If the owner of this store knew what his or her employee had just done, they would have been a different kind of hot. The employee tried to take money out of his owner's pocket.

Caveman Office Supply again — getting newsletters printed and nobody can figure it out

Before my newsletter list grew to a size that made it necessary to have them printed and sent from a mailing house, I had to use Caveman Office Supply for printing services. A special printer is required to print on 11x17 papers which are folded into booklet style. This is something we couldn't do it at the office.

When I first called the store to find out about the service, I was told that they could do it, but I had to physically bring in a thumb drive with the newsletter already created on a pdf. I couldn't just email the pdf because they had experienced "problems in the past." That was my hint that there were problems to come.

I arrived at the Headquarters and waited for a few minutes in the printing department. The guy called me up to the counter and took my order. After 11 minutes of trying to print my newsletters, he called for backup. A young lady came and took over the computer and showed the guy how to print my newsletters. It took special instructions to get it to print because they had a new program.

A month later, I went back to have newsletters printed again. This time the young lady wasn't there. My second hint; this smelled like trouble. Two guys took turns pushing buttons and shrugging their shoulders while looking at each other like a couple of cavemen simultaneously poking a porcupine and computing calculus. I chimed in and shared a few things that the young lady had said last month, but I couldn't explain it entirely. After all, *I* didn't work there. Finally they figured it out.

The next month I called ahead. This time I wanted to make sure that I wouldn't be stuck again while waiting for my newsletters. My time is valuable and I don't want to stand around watching cavemen confuse each other. I didn't say that, but I wanted to. I did explain that I often had to wait a long time. I asked, "Could I please send the pdf so that it would be done when I arrive?" They denied my request of convenience for everyone concerned, but they assured me that there would be no problem getting the program to work. When I arrived, sure enough — they couldn't figure it out. Luckily the young lady from a few months ago was there walking around the store. I called to the cavemen and pointed to her, "That's her. She knows what to do." She came over and got the print job going. Thankfully they didn't whack her over the head with one of their cattle bone clubs to win her heart.

I couldn't take it anymore so I spoke up. I said to all three of them, "Why don't you write down the steps she just explained and tape it to the side of the computer or save it somewhere else?" "That's a good idea," said the Fred and Barney wannabees; they proceeded to do nothing about it.

That was the last time I spent my money or wasted my time getting newsletters printed there. I happily paid more to get them done elsewhere at a place that didn't employ cave dwellers, and that accepted my emailed pdf and let me pick my goods up later.

Caveman Office Supply yet again — getting manuals printed

I will spare you the details of why I was in a hurry to get some advertising/marketing manuals printed. Unfortunately, my urgent need led me back to the place that hired cave dwellers. I was in a hurry, it was a different type of job, and it was a year later. *Certainly*, I reasoned, *they figured out how to print things by now.*

I came back to pick up the order and found that 17 out of 20 were obviously flawed on the front cover. I pulled out the damaged manuals and said I needed new ones printed. The employee *actually told me* that it was the best they could do with their equipment. I walked out, irritated and vowed never to buy from that place again.

All three of these stories reference one particular store's location. What happened there is a good argument for using secret shoppers. People continue to make the same mistakes and continually have to be checked on. Hopefully the business owner would see the pattern and do something about it.

Code Red Parcel* — trying to send an important package

All I wanted to do was mail a package and make sure it arrived at the destination on time. It was an essential package for a new client. Just before I paid, the employee said in a confiding manner, "You know, you don't need to send this with us for this type of package. You can go across the street to the post office and save money."

I thought back to the parts store scenario. This time I had to say something. I firmly said, "I need this package to get to my client on time. It's important."

Unbelievably the employee argued, "Oh, they will get it there on time and for less money — across the street."

I was polite, but explained, "It's too important to chance. I trust your company to get it there on time. I am paying for trust, not shipping."

Thankfully for the owner of the company, I won my argument with his employee and I was *allowed* to give them my money.

This employee didn't seem vindictive as if he wanted to hurt his employer. He sounded like he genuinely just wanted to be a nice guy and save me some money.

If the employees in any one of these stories had been soldiers, they would have been sent back to boot camp. Others may require a Blanket Party Code Red beating with bars of soap inside of a sock ala *Full Metal Jacket*. A few would earn a dishonorable discharge, and one or two would be treated as traitors for having committed treason, ala Benedict Arnold.

Daydream with me about an interrogation featuring the employees in my preceding stories...

Caveman Office Supply interrogation:

Caveman: "I helped him find the right paper. How was I supposed to know he needed a case of it?"

Interrogator: "Because that is what he had in his hand in the first place."

Caveman: "But he may have only needed one ream of paper and couldn't find it. I did get him the correct paper."

Interrogator: "Forget that you got him the correct paper. That's your job! So is maximizing our company's profits. Don't down-sell customers."

Caveman: "What's down-sell?"

Interrogator: "Ah, forget it."

That conversation with every employee whom I encountered would probably be similar. In every situation the employees were friendly, although clueless. As an employer, how can you make sure that you don't have cavemen representing your business to valued customers? My advice:

Buying paper at Caveman Office Supply

In this situation, the employee needed to pay more attention — or he needed training. Probably both. It's not likely that he failed to notice that I originally approached him with an entire case of paper in my hands. He may have thought that I only needed one ream but couldn't find it. He should have asked. Regardless, he should have tried to determine how he could sell me the case if I only had one ream to begin with. If he'd asked, he would have found out that I own a business and that I am not printing for personal use. He would have learned that I go through a *lot* of paper.

Employees without training may think that if I only had one ream of paper to begin with, they should grab one ream of paper. An untrained employee won't understand that not only is it in the store's best interest to sell me more, it may be in *my* best interest. Running out of paper is a problem for my business. What if I ran out of paper and stores were closed? What if my shipment came a day late? I would be stuck sending someone from my team to get paper from a store, wasting their valuable time at my expense. It actually costs me less money to have extra paper in the first place. Although a case of paper is more expensive overall, the cost per ream of paper is less than buying one ream at a time.

The debacle of printing newsletters at Caveman Office Supply

The incident where employees didn't know how to print my newsletters the first time is forgivable. If they had pride in their jobs they would have learned how to use the system when they realized the system had changed. After it happened a second time, they should have written it down so that everyone would know how to print the newsletters.

Aside from the newsletter debacle, I was peeved at not being allowed to send the pdf ahead of time. That is ridiculous. It is probably a management decision or a systems issue. For me, it was a total inconvenience. An overwhelming percentage of people who use their services probably are business owners or people in management positions. These types of customers are usually pressed for time. Having a convenient method to order print jobs would allow the office company to cater to busy business people.

Printing manuals at Caveman Office Supply

Trying to pass off flawed manuals demonstrates a lack of pride in their work. This is like a restaurant server bringing out a piece of fish that looks like a charcoal briquette on a plate and telling the customer, "Sorry. That is the best we can do."

The Wonky Auto Parts employee who told me to drive another few blocks to save money

This is the equivalent of being a traitor to your company. The employee would likely defend himself and claim that he tried to save someone money; he was looking out for the customer. Well, it's not his job to save the customer money by sending them to a competitor. It is the employee's job to offer what is in the store where they work. If the customer wants to buy where you work and pay more, let them. Don't talk them out of it.

Employees should know better in this case, but training still does some good. I don't know if the battery that I purchased was just as good as the one I would have purchased at Walmart or not. It may have been exactly the same. I didn't care. I was tired from church and teaching and taking care of 21 five-year-olds. It was hot outside. I wanted to pay for convenience and to save time.

Code Red Parcel employee telling me to go across the street to save money

This was another traitorous employee sending a customer to the enemy (competitor.) It is likely that this employee dislikes the ownership or leadership. He considers himself to be on the same side as me in a battle against the evil empire — The Business.

The never-ending book

There are hundreds of stories to share. During my research for writing this book, I asked a few friends about their bad service experiences. They could easily fill a 1,000-page book about poor service. These weren't just bad service stories. I purposely chose stories about employees who would probably argue in front of a Court Marshall that they were doing something good either for the customer or for the company.

A number of other problems to address include:

- Poor service
- Bad attitudes
- Theft
- Regression
- Laziness
- Lack of ambition
- Resentment

Fortunately, most employee challenges can be solved by a better hiring process, actions that you take as a leader, boot camp and surveillance.

Hire the right people in the first place

Money spent on weapons and technology plays a massive role in the strength of any country's military. Assessing one soldier to another soldier with all else being equal, the soldier who *wants* to be a soldier will be a better one.

Be careful — offering enough money with hopes to attract employees is equal to hiring mercenaries. Mercenaries can be useful but an employee who wants to do the job, *believes in* the job and gets paid for the job is a better employee. Mercenaries are in the job for personal reasons only as long as they want to be.

Your hiring process should consist of weeding out candidates. Simply speaking with applicants is not enough. Some people are great at interviews but make terrible employees. They are great at talking — good for an interview but doesn't always translate into work ethic.

The best scenario is to see an employee in action before they come to work for you. Send a spy on a reconnaissance mission and get a full report. Make sure the recruit is battle-tested. The next best mission is a tryout. Give an applicant something to do and see how they perform. In some instances due to regulations that may not be possible. But if you can give them a tryout, do so. It's not a good idea to only rely on a conversation to determine whom to hire.

Another good idea is to speak with your existing top guns. They may know other top guns who can be recruited to work for you.

Hire for integrity

It takes years to build a reputation and one moment to ruin it. Mistakes and poor service still get a second chance by customers, but if the employee has questionable integrity — you're done. Nobody wants to be taken advantage of, lied to, or cheated.

Unfortunately, people don't usually tell you that they are going to steal from you or your customers. It's not always easy to determine if someone has integrity.

I like what the boss, Mr. Tyson, did in the movie *Courageous* when looking for a manager of shipping and inventory. The manager called employee Javier Martinez up to his office. Tyson spoke about a new opportunity, but Javier would need to fudge the reports. He offered Javier time to think it over. Javier explained that he would love to have the job but would not lie on any reports. Tyson enticed Javier one more time and hinted that Javier's current job could be in jeopardy if he didn't take the promotion and lie on reports. Javier declined again, which prompted Tyson to stand up and shake Javier's hand. He told Javier it was an integrity test, and that out of six other people, he was the first person to pass.

Integrity is not something you teach on the job. Someone either has it or they don't.

Hire for personality

If the job opening is for someone who will communicate with any of your customers, then you should hire for personality.

Think about a time when you went out to eat and the server was "just there." The order was taken, the food came out on time and the bill was accurate. That is not a memorable experience that leads to repeat business. You often suffer the same experience when traveling. Once you are finally called up to a ticket counter, the customer service agent takes your bag, checks you in and, "Next!" At a retail or grocery store it can be difficult to find someone who is smiling and truly having a great time.

My wife and I have had several enjoyable experiences at Trader Joe's. Everyone has always been friendly and helpful. They all seem to love their jobs and they like people. I once asked a manager at the Trader Joe's that we frequent, "How do you do your hiring? What do you look for first? Is it personality?" The manager said, "Yes we definitely look for happy people with personality."

In one memorable example, my wife and I went into Trader Joe's after church. Dona, an employee, said, "Hello," as always. She added, "You don't normally come in on Sundays." I was impressed that she remembered what day we normally come in. We had spoken to her on a few occasions but someone paying close attention to our shopping habits is not something we normally experience. I told Dona that it was our wedding anniversary and we were picking up some wine and dinner for the night. She gave us a big smile and seemed to be genuinely happy for us. She didn't just say, "Happy Anniversary!" She asked us, "How many years?" She dug deeper for information and made us feel special. The best moment came when we checked out and started to head out the door. Dona came over with a bouquet of flowers. She handed them to us and said, "Happy Anniversary!"

I was shocked. You just don't see that kind of service or interest anywhere. It was good enough for me that she was friendly and happy for us when we were looking for dinner items. She went above and beyond by taking a genuine interest in us as people.

More companies should encourage their employees to take such an interest in their customers.

It's smart to hire for intelligence

Carl Sewell from Sewell Automotive and author of *Customers for Life* advises to hire for intelligence. A happy employee with a good personality who isn't capable of doing his job well won't be a happy employee for long. Ideally, you want both — personality and intelligence. I agree with Sewell that an intelligent team makes things easier. Eventually something will happen at work that was not part of employee training. An employee will have to rely upon their intelligence and good judgment to make a good decision on behalf of your company. Don't be afraid to hire people who are smarter than you.

Match skills to the job

Fighter pilots fly fighter jets. They don't drive Army tanks. People are put in a position of strength, otherwise people will suffer. Put your employees in positions where they can thrive. Don't take them out of a position where they are already good at something and put them into a completely different position. If the pilot is great they may be promoted to Top Gun but they shouldn't be promoted to Tank Commander. In case you are not up on your military jargon, another way to put it is that the power hitter on a major league baseball team will be out of place as a batting coach teaching little guys how to hit home runs.

Systems and processes keep things organized

Even a team member with a glowing personality can experience frustration if thrown into a mess with no systems to keep things running smoothly. Most people do better following a system. Imagine the chaos in a restaurant if tables and sections weren't divided up or if all the servers placed food and drink orders according to personal taste. Some use a computer to put an order in and others hand a ticket to the chef. When everyone follows one process it gives you an opportunity to test new ideas and tweak the method. Broken links in the chain are easier to find and fix if everyone follows the procedures that have been laid out.

Put ideal customers in front of your team

An ideal customer who is a perfect fit for your business is more likely to be happy. Your marketing that attracts customers to your business will affect the service and happiness that the customer feels.

Again using a restaurant as an example, if you spend your advertising budget to fill your steak house with vegetarians, you won't have many happy customers. You will have some, because there are two items on the menu for vegetarians. Truthfully, that is not an experience most people want to have. Continually putting the wrong customers in front of your team will deflate your team.

Make everyone a better salesperson

I may be biased about working hard because my first full-time job as a teenager was in a restaurant. I worked for tips for a number of years to make ends meet. Some people I worked with toiled as hard as they could all of the time, but I was surprised to see that some people were happy to do as little as possible. After several years of working in the restaurant business, I realized that some people are just lazy, but others need training about how to sell the product.

Effective selling could have them driving a luxury vehicle instead of a tailpipe-rattling heap of metal.

I know a server named Martin who specialized in gourmet. Martin thinks of himself as a sales person. He said, "Every time I sell a bottle of water I make a $1.60 tip. If I sell 10 bottles per night, that's $16 in tips just for water! That's $90 per week, $360 per month, $4,320 per year. I get to drive a nice new car instead of a junker — just because I sell extra water to the table."

Everyone should get the Martin training. Most servers in this situation only think about the extra buck or so. They don't calculate long-term benefits. They certainly don't consider what that extra $1.60 at a time could do to improve their lives.

A salesperson's goal of selling more to make more is in line with your business goals, but what about a non-commissioned employee?

Carl Sewell believes in performance-based pay for everyone. His sales people do get performance pay, but he also comes up with creative ways for each employee to benefit. I agree — when it is possible. Training should teach your employees that everyone affects sales revenue. In essence, everyone is a salesperson. Performance pay for non-sales employees can be based upon behaviors such as number of phone calls or appointments made. Break down individual tasks that an employee should get done in a day and set daily limits.

A word of caution→ Payment plans are meant to lead to a desired result by influencing behavior. Make sure your payment plan does not encourage employees to skip critical behaviors for short-term gain. Employees tend to think short-term while ownership thinks long-term. This is normal. You plan on owning the business for 20 years, but employees may not think past working on your team for more than two years — even if they like working at your business.

Empower employees for your good

You would think a business owner was looking down the barrel of an assault rifle when told to empower employees. The commonly held belief is that they will release all control to a group of after-hours drunken misfits who want to drive combat tanks capable of extreme destruction.

Empowering employees doesn't mean letting them run wild. I have a private client who allows employees to use their best judgment to make a customer happy *up to* $100; the key words there are *up to*. The owner has given employees some power, but not the keys to the Panzer tank. This does three important things:

1 - It increases the chances that the customer will be made happy quickly. Speed matters. Think about how many times you have been in a situation where the decision to be made by the business is obvious — such as a refund — but you have to wait while they, "Check with management."

2 - It frees ownership to focus on creative tasks or strategize or relax. I've been to business events and training workshops that cost each person several thousand dollars to attend. At these events I see business owners texting their staff and scampering out of the room to call their team and make a decision that no one else is allowed to make. They spend thousands of dollars to attend a workshop but have constant distractions because too many decisions can only be made by the owner.

3 - It engages your team. The more you make your employees feel like they are an important part of the company, the more they will perform. According to Gallup's State of the American Workplace: 2010-2012 report, estimates are that actively *disengaged* employees cost the U.S. $450 billion to $550 billion in lost productivity per year. To the contrary, when employees are engaged, you can expect:

 * 37% lower absenteeism

 * 25% lower turnover (in high-turnover organizations)

 * 65% lower turnover (in low-turnover organizations)

 * 28% less shrinkage

 * 48% fewer safety incidents

 * 41% fewer patient safety incidents

 * 41% fewer quality incidents (defects)

 * 10% higher customer metrics

 * 21% higher productivity

 * 22% higher profitability

In addition to decision-making power, involving your team in planning and developing new ideas will keep them engaged and empowered. Teach your team how to fish versus handing them a fish. Unless you want to reside at your business, your team needs to figure things out. They need to be able to make decisions and answer questions that aren't in the company handbook.

Leadership — talk about your customers as if they are listening

Leaders must lead when customers are watching *and* when they are not. Water cooler conversations about how some customers are a pain is detrimental to the company in general. Leaders cannot condone this or be a part of it. Trying to buddy up to employees while they privately bash your customers — leads to failure. It is better to explain to the team how important it is to find something to appreciate about customers even when they are difficult.

Did you know that babies only 12-hours old will imitate people by sticking out their tongues?[26] In the same way, employees will imitate leadership's attitude toward customers. Your team may think that they can bash customers privately, yet publicly treat them like they are important. But someone always knows. It can't be faked forever.

Some actors make $10 million dollars in a movie but the movie still stinks, as does the acting. If a "professional" actor practices their entire life, gets paid $10 million and still does a poor job of being convincing, how can you expect your team to pretend to appreciate customers if they are always criticizing them?

Addressing the big four deflating attitudes

Attitude #1 - Our job isn't important; All we do is sell "X"

A Workplace Dynamics study of roughly 1 million Americans revealed two things employees most want in the workplace: the first is *To be excited about the direction of the company*. If an employee is not invested in where the company is headed or what the company stands for, then they're only there for a paycheck. Surveys have shown that a paycheck in and of itself is not motivation for hard work.

Attitude #2 - The owner doesn't appreciate us

According to the Workplace Dynamics study, the second thing employees most desired in the workplace was *To feel appreciated for their contribution.* When employees don't feel appreciated they become disconnected and mentally check out. Employees want to love their company and for their company officials to appreciate them.[27] [28]

Attitude #3 - The owner makes too much money

There has been a public uproar about CEOs making 30 times what their employees make. Yet no one complains about LeBron James making 100 times more than a locker room attendant.

People don't *see* everything the CEO or owner has gone through to get where they are. No one sees their years of struggle and the 100-hour work weeks or the sleepless nights. They don't see family challenges that come with being a business owner. They don't see the business owner negotiating with vendors. As the business grows, employees don't see the owner struggling to hire more people such as accountants, attorneys, or crews that come after-hours to clean up the mess.

Attitude # 4 - The owner doesn't pay us enough

You have gone through the struggles of growing a business. You may have spent millions of dollars and thousands of hours getting the business to where it is today. Your value to the company doesn't change your team's value to the company. Money isn't everything as mentioned earlier, but it is relevant — especially when it comes to good employees.

Trying to replace good employees stinks, so pay them accordingly while providing a thriving environment.

Overcoming the big four deflating attitudes

While writing this section on the big four deflating attitudes I considered listing each one individually and immediately following it with a solution. I chose to offer solutions lumped together because the truth is, some of what I share below can have a positive impact on one or all of the big four deflating attitudes.

In addition, attitudes #3 and #4 may only be a problem because #1 and #2 are a big problem.

Purpose

Get employees excited and bought into what the company stands for, and they will enjoy the journey and deliver more effort in getting there. People need a purpose, and it needs to be more than a paycheck. You may need to explain it to them. A used car dealer who works with people who have bad credit doesn't just sell cars and charge high interest rates. They may be the only option that a family has to get Dad to and from work. They may be the only option for parents to get little Billy to Little League baseball practice.

Genuine appreciation

I was once an employee at a business that had an authoritarian general manager. He was intelligent and worked extremely hard. As an employee, I was privy to some things that employees did and said when he wasn't watching. Employees worked hard as long as he watched them. When he wasn't there (which was rare) their work ethic changed. I did not approach him with a list of lazy employees but I did sit down with him and explain that employees did not feel appreciated. He said, "I am not going to show appreciation for someone doing their job. It's their job. They are supposed to do it."

I agree; everyone should do their job. If they did, there wouldn't be a need for managers and coaches. If you want to get the most out of your employees, show genuine appreciation for them. Do not compare their work ethic or passion for the business to yours. There is a reason you own the business. Some people don't want to own a business and there is nothing wrong with that — but don't compare them to you. You don't have to walk around handing out bonuses to people who are simply doing their job, but a genuine, "Good job today," will increase the likelihood that the same person will do a good job tomorrow.

Share stories

If you have never told your story, many of your employees probably think that your parents handed you the business and your life was smooth sailing. Or they think you got lucky and are an overnight success. They don't appreciate you.

Tell your story. Share your initial struggle. Tell them how proud you are of your company and of them. They represent your good name and you expect that they will do a great job. When you share your story, you humanize yourself. If a family member handed down your business, your struggle may not be as powerful — so tell your family story. Employees at Disney and at Ford Motor Company know each founder's story.

Tell customer success stories and share testimonials with your entire company. If you have a small enough organization, share a customer success story or testimonial at the start of each day. If you have a larger organization and this is not possible, you should have an internal communication system that allows you to share positive stories. Combine this communication with employee appreciation by highlighting employees in an internal company newsletter.

Insider secrets

Share more about the inside business with your employees. They will appreciate you and your business more. Your employees often look at gross sales and not the net. They don't know about all of the fees and expenses that you have to pay. It's up to you how much you share, but I can tell you that I have rarely seen businesses that share enough insider information with their employees.

One division of your company may not appreciate another division. Give them a chance to experience what the other division does. As a young man when I worked at the Hard Rock Café in Las Vegas, I was able to see how valuable this experience was. Part of the training as a food server was spent working in the kitchen where line cooks worked hard keeping up with orders. As part of the training team, I had the pleasure of instructing management from all over the world. Part of that program was to spend time working in every position inside the restaurant.

Don't confuse this practice with cross-training employees to cover for each other. I never once saw a manager jump behind the line to flip burgers.

This aspect of training at the Hard Rock Café was to develop team appreciation.

Don't be a socialist

Reward your best with higher pay. Good employees resent the socialist payment plan of paying everyone the same because "it's fair." Well, it's *not* fair, not to the best employees anyway. If paying your best people more leads the lesser-paid to quit, who cares? You can find plenty of average employees. Replacing your best employees is more difficult.

Relax while taking a day off

Implementing what I have shared with you in this chapter increases the likelihood that your team will enjoy working for you and they will have a sense of purpose. This leads to greater production and a more impactful company. It also gives you the opportunity to have a day off and not have to worry that your business will fail while you enjoy a time of rest.

CHAPTER 6

Boot Camp — Training

Question: *What if we put a lot of money into training an employee — then they leave?*

Answer: *What if you **don't** train an employee and they stay?*

Boot Camp, also referred to as "Recruit Basic Training" is six to 13 weeks of extremely intense military training.

According to Military.com, Boot Camp will help you develop into a mature, highly disciplined, and fully capable armed forces service member if you have the courage to succeed. During this time, Drill Instructors (DIs) teach recruits how to care for themselves and others, function as a team member, and how to achieve success together.

Read that last paragraph again. Consider how many businesses are stocked with employees who are not highly disciplined, fully capable, or able to function as team members.

If you have hired the right people and have followed the principles put forth in the last chapter, it is time to send your troops to Boot Camp to prepare them for battle. Your "camp" should include the following topics:

Understand the product and service

This one seems obvious. However, there are times that I have visited or telephoned a business and the person I speak with knows less than I do after my 15 minutes of online research. I have often found that the employee cannot answer even basic questions. Customers want to be comfortable when parting with their money. The person they deal with should know what the heck they are talking about. While travelling for speaking gigs I sometimes call the hotel and ask someone at the front desk basic questions that they often don't have answers to: *What kind of food is served in the restaurant? How late is the business center open?*

Why people buy

Your team should understand not only what people buy, but WHY people buy. You also need to know this so that you can teach it. Reasons people buy are often different than what you think. As an entrepreneur, you are proud of your product or service and want to believe that people buy from you because yours is the best. That may be true. And it may be something else. Figure out what it is and teach it. This is also information you should use to sell your product or service.

In the previous chapter, you read the story about an employee telling me that I could go a few miles down the road to save $10 on a car battery. In my mind, I wanted to pay for a battery **and** *convenience*. He didn't get the second part.

People buy for many reasons, such as:

- Solutions — to fulfill a need.

- Prestige — it makes them feel good to buy; purchasing status.

- Save time — it saves time to buy.

- Convenience — it is easier to buy than the alternative.

- Speed — it is faster than the alternative.

Knowing reasons why people are willing to open their wallets will help your employees get over the fact that there may be cheaper options elsewhere.

Why people buy from YOU

- Credibility — People trust your character and integrity.

- Trust your ability — People believe you have the ability to deliver on your promises.

- Prestige — It makes them feel good to buy from you. You are the "go to" person. It gives people a story to tell their friends when they buy from you.

- Time savings — It saves time to buy from you than to go searching elsewhere.

- Convenience — It is easier to buy from you based on location or the purchasing process.

- Relationship — People buy from someone they know, like and trust.

- Timing — You are available and on their minds when others aren't.

- Price — When everything above is missing, people rely upon price to make their purchasing decision.

Years ago, my dad was a construction carpenter and was promoted to foreman. After years of overseeing production of multi-million dollar homes and projects, he was asked by some of those homeowners to hang Christmas lights. These people who lived in ultra-affluent households were willing to pay top dollar.

I've seen my dad's carpentry work, and it's top-notch. However, when it comes to hanging a few strings of Christmas lights, there are hundreds of people who can do that just as well as my dad. But the biggest reason these homeowners paid premium prices for my dad to do a "simple" job was because they trusted him with the keys to their homes.

Being trustworthy is normal to Dad, so in his mind, it was no big deal. I am not even sure if he knows why those wealthy homeowners didn't pay someone else 50 percent less than what they paid him. These homeowners had $100,000 cars in their garages, $50,000 watches, and $20,000 diamond earrings. Those homeowners paid for trust. Trust inflates price.

If you offer a commodity, people will buy based upon lowest price. Give them other, better reasons to buy from you.

Reasons customers pay a premium

To some extent, every reason listed under *Why people buy from YOU* are reasons that people will pay a premium. Here are a few more:

Pay a premium for a story

If customers know the story behind a product or service, they will pay top dollar. At high-end restaurants, gourmet servers tell how white truffles are only found in a few places on Earth, such as in the town of Alba, Italy. These truffles are sniffed out by truffle hogs. The pigs have a good sense of smell and will identify truffles from as deep as three feet underground. It is thought that male pigs' natural sex hormones are similar to the scent of truffles. Pigs also have a natural affinity for rooting the earth for food. Using swine to hunt truffles dates back to the days of the Roman Empire.[29]

I experienced first-hand the pungent odor of truffles. Someone had dropped a bottle of truffle oil at the casino restaurant I worked at, and it was so strong that I had to convince security not to call the fire department. The broken bottle released a distinct aroma that permeated throughout the building. The security team said they had fielded multiple reports of a gas leak.

Pay a premium to be able to tell their own story

Attendees at events where celebrities perform or make an appearance will pay extra to go backstage or meet the superstar. They get a picture, too — not so they can stare at it and remember their 10 seconds with a famous person. They want to show off the picture and tell the story about what happened during those incredible 10 seconds. They boast to their friends by telling their "insider" or "entertaining" story about their experience that could only be had because they paid a first-class price.

Pay a premium to flaunt their purchase

In the movie *The Bucket List*, Jack Nicholson's character is shocked when Morgan Freeman's character gives him details about how his coffee of choice is created. In a Sumatran village where the special beans are grown, wild tree cats eat the beans and poop them out. The poop is scooped, and voila! Kopi Luwak, the world's most expensive coffee, is ready to be brewed and consumed…after the beans are rinsed off and dried, of course. For a mere $249, you too can sip 12.3 ounces of this delicious coffee.

Exclusivity

Add the words *Limited Edition* to just about anything and the price goes up. Rolls Royce is a great vehicle as far as I know. I've been inside a Rolls but I haven't driven one. The manufacturers only release a limited amount — that fact drives the price up.[30]

Disney releases movie DVDs for a limited time and then puts them back into a vault. This strategy has worked for years. Imagine what havoc would ensue in your home if your kid found out that you had a chance to buy a *Frozen* DVD but you waited too long and then poof! It was gone.[31]

All economic levels

These examples of why people will pay more are not just for the wealthy. People at all economic levels want what they want regardless of economic status. Consumers with lower incomes stand in line to pay extra for the next gadget when their current gadget is working just fine. In the poorest of neighborhoods there are satellite dishes on rooftops.

Train your employees for more than what they will encounter

May 1st, 2011; Operation Neptune Spear was under way. An hour and a half into the mission, the first Blackhawk with call sign "Chalk One" was supposed to hover over a compound and drop two fast ropes for SEALs to slide into a courtyard. Instead, the helicopter fish-tailed and soft crash-landed into the wall with its nose buried in the dirt. The pilot for the second Blackhawk with call sign "Chalk Two" saw what happened to Chalk One and made a quick decision to land outside of the compound that contained Osama Bin Laden.[32]

The carefully rehearsed plan was out the window before the first SEAL exited a Blackhawk.

SEALs train for all types of situations that they may never encounter. They are trained to handle the unexpected. That is exactly what SEAL Team 6 did. Years of training and weeks of rehearsals on a full-size North Carolina version of Bin Laden's Abbottabad, Pakistan compound led to a successful mission.

Of course, a comparison of your workplace or your employees to a Navy SEAL is extreme. These are some of the most physically and mentally tough people on Earth. Because of their efforts, you can own your business in a free country. In fact, their efforts allow me to freely write this book. I use SEALs as an example because it is valuable to study the best of the best in all areas of life. Take that information and adjust it to levels that make sense. Take lessons learned from studying the best and formulate a plan. Pick up ideas such as:

The real thing

It is better to over-prepare and train your employees than to under-train them. Teach your employees how to handle the unexpected. Instruct your employees how to work as a team so they can pick each other up just as SEALs do. Replicate business situations so that handling issues in certain ways becomes second nature to your team. Having a company manual and studying it is important, but practicing as close to the real thing as possible will have your team better prepared.

Basic phone skills would be nice

Call a new employee and see how they handle a question that they don't know an answer to. There is no doubt that will happen at some point. Rather than giving them one million answers, teach them how to respond when they *don't* know the answer. A number of times I have asked an employee a question and they didn't know the answer. I have either received attitude or a quick, "I don't know," that was NOT followed up with a, "but I will find out." I've spoken to several people who have had the same experience on multiple occasions.

Train continuously

SEALs don't go to BUD/S (Basic Underwater Demolition/SEAL) training and wait for action. They continue to prepare so that when any moment comes, they are ready.

There is hope out there

When you implement principles learned from the last chapter and put your team through Boot Camp or BUD/S training, you will set up your company for success. Here are a few examples:

Manager makes a smart business decision

My wife made a shopping trip to Costco. She had a number of items on her list including a software program that I needed. On the way home she cheerfully called and said, "I got your program." She turned to look in the back seat and didn't see it. All of a sudden she couldn't remember if she had actually purchased it. So she pulled over and said she'd call me back. My wife looked at the receipt and sure enough, the software charge was on there. She looked in the trunk and everywhere else but the software box was nowhere to be found. In a panic, she called me back saying, "I bought the software, I can't find it anywhere — I think I left it in the basket; I didn't put it in the car." Through a series of deductions, she knew she hadn't left it in the store. She remembered seeing it in her cart while she was in the parking lot. My wife decided to go back to the parking lot to look for it and hope that someone turned it in. Meanwhile, I called Costco and spoke to a manager. I told him what happened. He said that no one had turned anything in, but he offered to send someone out to check the carts.

After scouring the Costco lot, my wife was empty-handed. I called the manager again and asked him to check the inside desk area one more time because my wife did not find the software box outside. After looking, he assured me that, "No, nobody has turned it in but I will call you if somebody finds it."

Not long afterward, the manager called me again. He said, "We didn't find the software program but you know what? Tell your wife to come into the store and see me. We'll give you another software program at no charge."

This wasn't even a gray area. The missing software was not Costco's fault. The manager wasn't obligated to do anything for us and I would not have been upset that he didn't. My guess is that the manager looked at our account and saw how much money we have spent over the years. He probably thought, *"This is an opportunity to take one of our happy customers and make them extremely happy."* His action turned us into marketing soldiers for Costco.

If that is what he thought — he was right. I have told that story many times. A Costco employee may have even found our software program later and turned it in, so it may not have cost them a thing. Either way, it was a smart move on the manager's part.

Proud to work here

My friend Jim Jackson, a business coach from JimJacksonLive.com shares a story from one of his clients:

An employee from a car dealership stood in a checkout line at a grocery store. She overheard a woman behind her talking to a friend about her car that had just broken down. The troubled woman said that she didn't have good credit and wasn't sure if she would be able to get financing for another vehicle. The dealership employee turned around and said, "I overheard your conversation. I work at a dealership that specializes in financing for people with less-than-perfect credit. I am not a sales person, but just come on in and we'll take care of you."

The take-away here is that you have an employee off-the-clock, promoting the business with no thought of personal monetary gain. She believes in the company she works for. She is proud to work at the dealership.

A restaurant

On our way back from vacation, my wife and I stopped at Chick-fil-A. We had our yellow Labrador Retriever with us so went through the drive-through. Unlike most drive-through speaker voices, the words coming through the speaker rang with happiness. The order-taker sounded happy to be there and happy to take our order. We received the same friendly service at the window. "Have a great day!" she said as we drove away.

I pulled into a parking spot so that my wife and I could eat our chicken with one of the many sauces that the smiling girl at the window gave to me. Before my wife finished eating, she remembered that she wanted to get a stuffed animal cow for her friend who is a super fan of Chick-fil-A. My wife stayed in the car with our dog while I went inside and requested the cow holding the "Eat Mor Chikin" sign. The cashier who helped me inside was just as friendly and happy as the girl at the drive-through window. I looked around and noticed that everyone sported the same friendly smile and attitude. Amazed, I walked out with the cow professing that people should "Eat mor chikin."

I am not the only happy customer to rave about the service at Chick-fil-A. Research survey group Zogby Analytics collaborated with 24/7 Wall St. to poll adults about the quality of customer service in 15 industries. The survey asked if service was "excellent," "good," "fair" or "poor." Those with the highest percentage of "poor" rankings make up the Customer Service Hall of Shame; those with the highest "excellent" ratings are in the Customer Service Hall of Fame.

Chick-fil-A was the sole restaurant in the 2014 Customer Service Hall of Fame. The only one. It ranked fourth — behind Amazon, Hilton, and Marriott.

The chain's employees appear to be satisfied as well. In 2014, Chick-fil-A was rated one of the best companies to work for by Glassdoor.com.[33]

An airline — (No, I'm not kidding)

According to the J.D. Power 2015 North America Airline Satisfaction Study[SM], airlines most focused on providing a pleasant experience for travelers are being rewarded with higher customer satisfaction and loyalty. The J.D. Power study measures passenger satisfaction amongst both business and leisure fares of major carriers in North America.

The study is based upon responses from 11,354 passengers who flew on any major North American airline between March 2014 and March 2015; it was fielded between April 2014 and March 2015.

Passenger satisfaction with North America airline carriers was measured using seven factors of performance. In order of importance: cost and fees; in-flight services; boarding/deplaning/baggage; flight crew; aircraft; check-in; and reservation.

Alaska Airlines ranked highest in the traditional carrier segment for an eighth consecutive year. The Seattle-based airline performs especially well in all seven factors of the study.[34]

A shoe company

"To build the Zappos brand into being about the very best customer service, we needed to make sure customer service was the entire company, not just a department" — from the book, *Delivering Happiness* by Tony Hsieh

With insight like this, it is no wonder that Zappos is known for exceptional customer service.

Zappos service and culture are so widely known that thousands of people per year tour the customer service department in Las Vegas. I've done it and can tell you that it is one of the most unique experiences I have ever had with touring a company during business hours. Our tour guide told me that Tony Hsieh considers customer service to be a *marketing* cost. More business owners should consider the tour guide's statement.

Your customers are part of your marketing team — *they* are your marketing soldiers. Word of mouth has always been the most powerful form of marketing. With today's technology, it is even more powerful. Your employees are part of your marketing team — because your customers are part of your marketing team.

When you make a mistake

With all the right systems in place, hiring the right people and hosting boot camp, there will still be mistakes.

An unhappy customer who can be turned around to happiness tells more people about your company than one customer who is happy to begin with. Now, I don't recommend trying to displease customers just to make them happy afterward. That is a dangerous gamble. But when you do make a mistake, react quickly to correct it.

1 - Acknowledge that you messed up and apologize. — Say, "I apologize," instead of, "I am sorry." Jeffrey Gitomer does a good job of explaining this difference in his book, Customer Satisfaction is Worthless, Customer Loyalty is Priceless. Gitomer wrote, "'I'm sorry' describes you and your state of being, not your circumstance. 'I apologize' tells how you feel about the circumstance."

Nobody wants to hear excuses or blame-shifting. As far as the person in front of you is concerned it's *your* fault. The upset customer may not care whose fault it is; only that they want it fixed **yesterday** and they want someone to own up to the problem.

In a *Wall Street Journal* article in 2004, Michael Woods, author of *Healing Words: The Power of Apology in Medicine*, wrote, "Nothing is more effective in reducing liability than an authentically offered apology." Woods teaches seminars for doctors and malpractice insurers about the importance of an apology.

2 - Fix it. — Some businesses encourage employees to ask customers, "How can we fix this for you?" in an effort to make sure that the issue at hand is solved exactly as the customer wants. This model may work for some, but the problem is that now you have left it up to the customer to figure out the solution. Think about it: you have messed up and now you want the customer to figure out the solution. How about you just fix the dang thing! Give the customer two options to choose from:

"We messed up and want to fix it. We can do 'A' or 'B.' Which do you prefer?"

Of course don't say it like a robot or exactly like you just read it. Say it as if you are a human talking to another human.

3 - Make sure that the customer believes that it was a one-time mistake. — If there is a broken system, get the system fixed. There is not much worse in the business world than recurring mistakes. Remember my story about the cavemen when I wanted my newsletters printed and nobody knew how to use the printer — AGAIN.

Invite the customer back to order again soon and assure them that the problem has been fixed and won't happen again. Send a "Thank You" card to the customer that states, "We want to thank you again for your business. We look forward to your next perfect encounter here."

After you make a mistake, your customer's mind wanders while they walk out the door. They wonder if they should try your competitor. They need to be certain that their next experience will be great.

Companies handling a mistake — crisis management

$100 million worth of crisis management

In 1982, seven people died after taking extra-strength Tylenol capsules that had been laced with potassium cyanide — a deadly poison.

Johnson & Johnson officials pulled 31 million bottles of Tylenol — $100 million worth — off shelves across the nation and stopped all production and advertising. They offered up to a $100,000 reward for information that led to finding the killer. The company put customer safety first.

After the crisis, Johnson & Johnson officials reintroduced Tylenol with tamper-resistant packaging and coupons worth $2.50 off the purchase price.

Media appreciated the lengths the company went to and their concern for the public's interest. This helped the Tylenol brand to recover trust. In college and university MBA classes worldwide, Tylenol's response to the crisis is still regarded as one of the most successful for crisis management.[35]

CEO issues personal apology

In 2009, Amazon higher-ups remotely deleted copies of George Orwell's books *1984* and *Animal Farm* from private readers' Kindles. The deleted versions were unauthorized. Amazon issued refunds. However, customers were angry because Amazon officials invaded personal devices and without warning or explanation took back content that had been legally purchased. The paid-for books inexplicably disappeared from devices while refunds showed up on accounts.

Six days later, Jeff Bezos issued this apology:

"This is an apology for the way we previously handled illegally sold copies of 1984 and other novels on Kindle. Our 'solution' to the problem was stupid, thoughtless, and painfully out of line with our principles. It is wholly self-inflicted, and we deserve the criticism we've received. We will use the scar tissue from this painful mistake to help make better decisions going forward, ones that match our mission.

With deep apology to our customers,

Jeff Bezos

Founder & CEO

Amazon.com"[36]

Some media articles referenced this as an Amazon-issued press release admitting that the company's actions were a mistake; however the fact that it was a personal apology from a human being is what calmed angry customers.

Skip the corporate dry babble and apologize. You are a human who interacts with other humans.

By the way, Amazon was ranked #1 for customer contentment by the American Customer Satisfaction Index for five years in a row from 2010 to 2014.

CHAPTER 7

Trust but Verify — Surveillance

Ronald Reagan said it best

Speaking in English and in Russian during a press conference on December 8, 1987 announcing the signing of the INF (Intermediate-range Nuclear Forces) Treaty with Russia, President Ronald Reagan astutely said, "Trust, but verify."

After you have done your utmost to hire the best people, have carried out ideas from Chapter 5, and your employees have been through boot camp and continued training — one thing left to do is, "Trust, but verify."

To monitor or not to monitor?

First, speak with your attorney and check the laws in your area before acting on any of the information and advice contained in this chapter. Also, do not drive with your car windshield sunshade in place — (aren't disclaimers silly?)

Six reasons to monitor your team:

1 - Look for time-wasters

A 2014 Salary.com survey revealed that 89 percent of people surveyed reported wasting time at work every day. That's up a whopping 20 percent compared to 2013. Here's the breakdown:

- 31% waste roughly 30 minutes daily
- 31% waste roughly 1 hour daily
- 16% waste roughly 2 hours daily
- 6% waste roughly 3 hours daily
- 2% waste roughly 4 hours daily
- 2% waste 5 or more hours daily

These stats reveal that 10 percent of people surveyed waste at least one-third of the average workday on non-work-related tasks.[37]

2 - Give your team a productivity boost

Every once in a while you might get a secret look at what your employees are doing, but I believe in letting them know that they are being watched for these reasons:

They are more likely to do things correctly in the first place.

Employees are more productive. During a study referenced in the book, *Why We Do What We Do*, by Edward L. Deci, observers discovered that employees were more productive when video cameras were installed — whether employees were being watched or not. The fact that they *thought* they were under observation was enough to increase production.

3 - Ensure compliance with following proper protocol and processes

Through trial and error, you have spent a lot of money and effort crafting optimum processes to maximize profits. Unwatched employees fall back into their own way of doing things, which is not tested and proven. I have personally witnessed this. During a consulting day with the business owner sitting next to me, I will sometimes disguise my phone number and call the business pretending to be a potential customer. At times my clients are horrified.

4 - Know where you need improvement

Consider my story earlier when buying paper. That employee probably needed training. His actions would not show up in receipts, performance evaluations or customer surveys. He was friendly. He did try to help me. His actions could only be corrected if someone witnessed his behavior and subsequent down-sell from my buying one case of paper to only one ream.

5 - Measure with the goal of improvement

When soldiers are training on an obstacle course or running great distances, everything is monitored and measured **all** of the time. Without monitoring results and activity, you leave performance up to the naked eye and subjective opinions. You can't improve what you don't monitor.

6 - As a theft deterrent

Employee theft and fraud costs U.S. businesses an estimated $20 billion to $50 billion each year.[38] Despite that huge number, most employees would not take money right out of the cash drawer. However, what about taking a pen, a pencil, or a ream of paper? One pen doesn't sound like a lot, but what if you have thousands of employees? It could cost you thousands of dollars each year. Employees who push customers out the door — like my story about trying to buy a car battery — are different kinds of thieves. It is not prosecutable, but it is costly.

What should you monitor?

Monitor anything you can count

Monitor everything that is easily measurable as well as things that take more effort to measure.

When you monitor as many things as possible, you will find broken links in the chain. If you measure the amount of leads you get via your website versus the number of those leads who come in to your place of business versus the number of those who buy, you can make a number of important deductions.

For example: if you get a sufficient amount of leads on the front end but not enough sales on the back end, you won't know the problem unless you monitor behavior in the middle. If you have plenty of front end leads but not many that visit your location, then you may have a problem with whoever is making phone calls to invite those leads in. If you are getting plenty of your front end leads stepping into your place of business, then the problem is not your people working the phones. The issue may be with the people who work in your physical location who deal with your customer face-to-face.

Monitor behavior

Monitoring the numbers just mentioned can make it faster for you to get to the area in which there is a problem but it won't necessarily tell you specific issues. This is why you need to monitor behavior. What does your team say on the phone? What do their email interactions look like? What is the speed of follow-up? All of these and more - play a role in the successful sale.

How to monitor

The following are a few suggested methods and tools to monitor your employees, along with reasons why they are beneficial:

Video surveillance

a. *Safety* — Employees should be happy about that. This can protect you from burglars and from customers who make false claims against employees.

b. *Theft deterrent* — If your team knows they are under surveillance, they are less likely to steal in the first place. If they do, you have video. Your honest employees will appreciate surveillance to prove their innocence.

c. *Demonstration* — Sometimes employees truly think they are doing a good job. They really believe they are following the processes that you have laid out for them. The only way to prove that they are not is to show it to them or let them hear it. Sales trainer Roger Shepard from Rampage, Inc. records conversations. Afterward, trainees listen to it with him. After hearing themselves, sales people often realize that they need improvement.

Software monitoring

There are software tools that monitor your employees' every click of the keyboard and web browsing while using **work computers**. Work computers is emphasized here, because at work people are supposed to be working. The #1 time-waster at work is dilly-dallying on social media.[39]

Check your CRM

If you are serious about marketing, you probably have a Customer Relationship Management tool. Your CRM is used to communicate and keep track of communications with customers. It helps to keep your employees organized and reminded of necessary communications. You should be checking the CRM to make sure it is being used.

On occasion I encounter an owner or person in leadership at a company who tells me, "I can't get the employees to use the CRM." This typically happens for one of three reasons:

1. Leadership doesn't clarify that it is NOT optional — it is part of the job.

2. The CRM is complicated to use; instructions or training didn't make it easier.

3. Employees don't realize the value of the CRM tool. Your employees should be trained how to use the CRM and *why*.

Communications monitoring

"This call may be recorded for quality assurance purposes." Countless times I've heard this message when calling customer service at a business — and then proceeded to get terrible customer service. It used to be shocking until I started consulting for businesses that used this message and found out that the owner didn't listen to ANY of the calls. Earlier I mentioned a study that discovered that people are more productive when they know they are being watched. Similar results may hold true when employees on the phone know they will be listened to — but you *must* listen to the calls every so often and let it be known that you do.

Secret shoppers

Surveillance alone may not catch everything that you need to know. This is where secret shoppers come in. To be most effective, employees should know that you commonly use secret shoppers to ensure that processes and systems are followed and that good service is given.

If you are trying to catch a thief or something equally dramatic, you may keep it a secret for a while — but secret shoppers are not only used to catch the dishonest. The fact that employees know that the next person on the phone or standing in front of them could be a secret shopper should motivate them to follow company instructions and give good service.

When you get a *shoppers report,* it should be reviewed in front of the entire staff. Employees who receive great *shopper reports* should be rewarded in front of everyone. Negative *shopper reports* should be used for training and employment decisions. Reviewing these reports in front of the entire workforce lets the team know that their work is being watched and reviewed. It is also your opportunity to reward the behavior that you want more of.

Recruit customers to assist in the monitoring process

Every business should have a customer feedback system. A direct line of communication from customers to ownership should be put in place. Give patrons an easy method for offering their feedback. Twenty-question surveys have a low response rate; they take too long to fill out. Cards that are handed to customers for comments that are to be given back to that same employee are often left blank; people don't want confrontation with the worker that they want to complain about. It is imperative to get feedback right away while their experience is fresh in their minds.

Employees should not be in charge of handling customer feedback. For example, if restaurant management requires that servers leave response cards on the tables they tend, they shouldn't expect the waitperson to put those filled-out cards in their pockets and blindly turn them all in at the end of their shift. Positive response cards will make their way to managers while negative cards will be thrown in the trash.

When setting up your feedback system, consider every possible option an employee can use to sabotage it. Explain to employees that the feedback system is meant to keep small issues from becoming big issues. Complaints can be handled internally instead of publicly -- public venting is online graffiti that hurts your business. Having an effective feedback system will help you avoid negative word-of-mouth that is detrimental to your business. We'll pick up this topic in the next chapter.

Go to KennyTalks.com
for feedback systems tips and tools.

"Please remove all guns and gadgetry"

Flying around the country for consulting days or speaking gigs, I've had more airport pat-downs than I care to count.

You will probably get a letter from an attorney if you do workplace pat-downs. However, you may be able to keep a list of their cell phone numbers and randomly call them while they are working and see whose pocket starts ringing.

I believe that all employees should check their gadgets and cell phones into their locker or other secured place when they arrive to work. An employee should not need their personal cell phone while working. If your employees need mobile phones to perform their jobs, they should be provided company-issued cell phones with capabilities for work-related tasks only.

Perhaps you too have had the experience of entering a place of business and the first person you come into contact with is goofing around on their cell phone WHILE supposedly helping you. For example, while I checked in for a recent flight, the customer service agent was fooling around on her cell phone. She typed my info into the computer, typed something on her cell phone...back and forth. Another airline employee snickered with her while they did everything *except* their jobs.

No, you don't own your employees; but you do own their time and attention while they are on your clock.

Additional tips

Resist the urge to think that trust erodes when you monitor employees or that your workplace will be a miserable place with restrictions in place for electronics use. Great employees will stand out. If you reward them, they will *want to* work harder and be more effective. This shows your employees that monitoring them isn't because you are looking for someone to fire. You are looking for good behavior and an opportunity to improve how you train them. Good employees will appreciate that you are watching.

Understanding why people do what they do will also help you devise a productive work environment. Why do people waste time? Would you believe it's because they think it's productive? More than half (53 percent) of all those surveyed said that they waste time because they believe short breaks actually increase productivity. Boredom came in a distant second — 20 percent of people said they simply aren't interested enough in their jobs to pay full attention. Lack of incentive (8 percent), being unsatisfied with their jobs (7 percent), and not being paid enough (2 percent) also made the list.[40]

Correct quickly

If you are correcting a correctable behavior, do it quickly. Don't wait. Letting things slide leads to this scenario:

- You want employees to say ,"Welcome," but one employee decides to say, "Hello"
- "Hello" leads to, "Hi"
- "Hi" leads to, "Hey"
- "Hey" leads to, "What's up?"

- "What's up?" leads to, "Whassup?"
- "Whassup" leads to, "Yo"

This may seem far-fetched. But nearly every business owner has some process or rule that is so far off what he or she originally intended that they don't know how it got to that point — or how to get it back on track.

Now you must watch them when they are off work

Have you considered that employees are a representation of your business on **and** off the clock? Make sure you keep that fact in mind when hiring — and make sure employees understand it during your boot camp. Otherwise you could end up with a mess. There are numerous stories about employees who were fired after bashing the company they work for, saying derogatory things about customers, and just saying stupid things in general.

The best way to keep employees from making your company look bad while they are off work is to hire the right people in the first place — and to provide a great job. "Great" can mean a lot of things including interesting, fun, rewarding, etc. Your goal should not be for employees to *pretend* to like their job, but for them to *actually* like it. Just because you and your customers help your employees to put food on their tables does not mean they will talk kindly about either of you in a public forum.

There are also monitoring tools that allow you to monitor the Internet for your company name. Use them. It will help you to watch for positive and negative comments made by customers and employees.

Get rid of bad apples before disease spreads through the barracks

For some employees, even a Code Red threat of a beating with bars of soap inside athletic socks won't work. Bad employees cost businesses more than can be accounted for. Tony Hsieh of Zappos knows this. After new employees finish training, they are offered $2,000 to quit. Yes — $2,000 to quit right there on the spot. Hsieh knows that it will cost Zappos more than $2,000 to keep a bad employee.

Bad employees not only fail to provide a return on investment, they are a subtraction to your profits. They drive customers away and spoil the whole bunch of employees. Even good employees can be demotivated by bad employees — especially if they make the same amount of money.

Don't make the mistake of keeping a bad employee until you can find a good replacement. Get rid of them immediately or risk causing resentment and hostility with other employees.

Customers may buy from you the first time because of your awesome marketing, but they buy from you again and refer others to you because of *their experience*.

You might be thinking, *Why so many chapters and pages on employees?* Two primary reasons are:

Fancy marketing and advertising to get customers to your place of business will be short-lived if employees don't provide a great experience. The market is saturated. Media that used to work well is struggling. Acquiring a new customer by way of advertising is expensive — so once you got 'em…keep 'em.

Your employees are in direct contact with the most important division of your marketing team — which happens to be what the next chapter is about...

CHAPTER 8

Volunteer Soldiers

Per day: 3,000 — 5,000 advertisements.

According to some marketing experts, the average person is exposed to that many advertisements on a daily basis. If true, that is 1.09 million to 1.8 million per year.

For comparison:

- People send or receive an average of 41.5 text messages on a typical day.
- Those with cell phones make or receive an average of 12 calls per day.[41]
- Worldwide in 2015, there were 204 billion emails sent per day.[42]

According to information from the Bureau of Labor Statistics, the average person aged 15 years and older sleeps 8.8 hours per day — which leaves 15.2 hours per day of awake-time where you can advertise to them.

The average human attention span is 8.25 seconds. The average attention span of a goldfish is 9 seconds.[43]

The point? With attention spans shorter than a goldfish and a saturated electronics market with so many businesses and types of communications reaching your customer, it takes a lot of effort to acquire new customers. Once you *do* get their attention — earn their business. Do a better job of taking care of your customers, keep existing customers, earn repeat purchases, and earn referrals.

Customers are hard to come by. Customer acquisition cost is one of the highest in any business. That rate seems to be on the rise as the market becomes more saturated and roadblocks are put in the way such as regulations combined with *advertisement avoidance technology*.

Your list of customers is the number one asset you have. A number of highly successful entrepreneurs will tell you that if all but one thing was taken from them and they had to start over — they would keep their existing customers.

The first step is to really know your customer and how important they are

Without customers you don't have a business and your employees don't have a job

Your customers sign the owner's paycheck who in turn, signs employees' paychecks

Your customers have major influence over gaining new customers

Your business's sole existence depends upon your ability to make customers happy by satisfying their needs and providing a good experience.

The owner's name is on the employees' paychecks, but the customer's name is on the owner's paycheck. The owner's check is divided up among ownership, partners, and employees.

The reason your employees are so important and why so much coverage in this book is given about them is twofold: they either deal directly with your customer, or their efforts directly affect the customer's experience.

Could one customer complaint cost a company $180 million?

In January 2013, the success of Dave Carroll's online protest was used by the German television and news service Tagesschau to exemplify a new kind of threat facing corporations in the Internet age.[44]

The following is a transcript from an interview with Dave Carroll. Only minor edits were made for easier reading while keeping the integrity of the interview.

Kenny: Hi, this is Kenny Atcheson. In this interview and discussion, I'm speaking with someone who has a great story. He is an award-winning singer, songwriter, professional speaker, author and social media innovator from Halifax, Canada. When faced with a difficult customer service issue with United Airlines in 2009, he decided to share his story with the world. He uploaded a video to YouTube. After only four days, it earned over 1 million views. This You-Tube video entitled, "United Breaks Guitars," became an instant viral hit. Today, more than 150 million people have been introduced to his story. BBC News announced that for a time, the "United Breaks Guitars" video dropped the market cap of United Airlines by $180 million. On the line with me today is Dave Carroll, from DaveCarrollMusic.com. Dave I'd like to ask you a few questions. Are you ready to get started?

Dave: I sure am Kenny. Thanks for having me on.

Kenny: Great, we're glad to have you. Love the story. Dave, number one, while reading your book I discovered a lot of people helped you with the video for free after you told them why you were doing it. Why do you think so many people wanted to help you produce and launch the video at no cost to you?

Dave: Probably a couple reasons. Number one, the media first of all, paints "United Breaks Guitars" as a story of confrontation about the small guy taking on the big company in an angry confrontation. I've always maintained that it's a story of non-confrontation in the fact that I had all these people and friends of mine volunteer their time and effort and talent to make a quality product. Something that really sounded good and looked good was a testament to the fact that there wasn't really a lot of animosity and anger. It was quite the opposite, and people were happy to be a part of it because it was funny and it resonated with people, which brings me to the next reason — that everybody in the world has had a bad airline experience. In a sense, "United Breaks Guitars" has become a metaphor for customer change. It's sort of carrying the torch for affected customers everywhere.

Kenny: I felt the same way the first time I saw it, and then started thinking of it from a marketing perspective. But when I first saw it, it was as a consumer who's had bad customer service experiences like myself in a variety of areas. By the way, you mentioned funny — if anyone hasn't seen the video, you must watch it. It is hysterical. My favorite scene, Dave, is when you have the chalk outline and you put your hand on it. I guess you're an actor too now, because you played the part well.

Dave: What that shows is how little budget I had with acting ability of not just me, but everybody in front of the camera. My friends.

Kenny: Your grandmother and all your friends. That was great. Maybe a movie next for you, or maybe a movie series on TV.

Dave: I'm thinking musical. We've got three songs already, and I thought this would make a great musical. Something I'm seriously considering.

Kenny: I like that Dave. I live in Henderson, just outside of Las Vegas. The Smith Center in Las Vegas hosts a lot of Broadway shows and my wife and I have been to quite a few. I'll be your first customer.

Dave, I have a two part question. If United showed empathy, remorse, or interest in your problem from the very beginning, is it possible that you would not have launched the video, even if United did not offer you total compensation? Part two of that question: do you think the sooner a problem is handled, the less costly it is to the business?

Dave: Yes, I think so, for sure. The question regarding empathy: the whole idea with customer service is that you, as a company, can diffuse a potentially explosive situation by showing respect, by showing caring and a concern to do the right thing. In my case, I think I was very fair in what I had offered them. My offer, when they finally said they would do nothing, was actually not for the full value of the guitar. What I'd asked for from the company was only the value of the guitar in flight vouchers. It cost me $1,200 to fix the guitar to a reasonable state, and I asked them for $1,200 in flight vouchers, thinking that was a fair offer because it would offset future travel costs for me, and show me that my next experience with United wasn't going to be the same. It would actually cost them nothing, provided that there was one empty seat on the flight I would be using. It seemed like a fair offer, but they said, "No," to that. That was really frustrating in itself. Having this go on for all those many months was making the situation much worse. So, yes, I was already prepared to take less than what some people might have thought was fair, and that was frustrating.

The sooner the better, I guess, on the second part of the question. Absolutely, doing something within days is much preferable than half a year or a year later, because once "business representatives" position themselves as not looking to solve a problem, what they're doing is digging in, and that forces the person that they're trying to deal with to dig in as well. Then it creates a confrontational situation that didn't need to be confrontational at all. Most consumers, I believe, are reasonable and fair. In the case of an airline experience, they really just want to get to where they are going, with the things of value that they brought from home intact.

Kenny: When I first read in the book that you were willing to take travel vouchers, I thought, *I wouldn't*. I was frustrated along with you, and I don't know that I would have wanted to accept at that point. It did seem like you were willing to take less. I just thought of something else: one of my clients really helped his customer service and made some changes. He allows his employees to make an immediate decision — which will cost his company money — up to a certain dollar amount. He does put a limit on it because he doesn't want them to spend him broke. However, he gives them the opportunity, and empowers them with decision-making authority. In your travels, since the video and your fame has grown, and you've been invited to speaking engagements, have you found any examples like I just mentioned?

Dave: Yes, I think one of the big examples that I keep coming across — I believe it's the Ritz Carlton example; they empower their chambermaids and cleaning staff to solve problems instantly when the customer presents it to them, up to $1,000. That's a lot of money, but I guess they find that very rarely do the people actually go to $1,000. Most problems can be solved for very, very little, and sometimes not at all. It's just the fact that being a customer, knowing that everyone in the organization is empowered to help you, probably makes the people easy-going about things that they're not satisfied with. And there are more companies I'm coming across, as you say all the time, that are considering that. That's one of the things I took away, and I continue to learn from "United Breaks Guitars" myself, is that we are all connected with one another, and every organization, once they realize that they're employees, and the people who make their products are actually connected to every aspect of the business, maybe showing them more respect and empowering them more to care about the product and the service, is actually profit in the long run.

Kenny: After the launch of the video, United called and offered you $1,200 for the guitar repair, *and* $1,200 in travel vouchers. Twice of what you had originally asked for — and you declined. At this point, it seems like it became a cause with more than one person behind the cause, and not just a compensation issue. Is that true? And if so, is that what inspired you to continue on and push so hard?

Dave: They made that offer after about nine months of me trying and told they would do nothing. It took another seven months for the first video to go out. A lot of time had gone by without United doing anything. At that point when I made the vow to make all three videos, it wasn't a negotiation tactic. It ended up being my promise to do something when United promised they would do nothing. At that point I never really intended to accept any compensation, and it wasn't about getting money from them. It was about following through on my word.

When the video went viral, that was completely unexpected. They made the offer on the fourth day. I put the video up on Monday, and on Friday we had that conversation. Ironically, it was the same day that I had reached my goal of 1 million hits with all three videos combined; here it was, with the first video after only four days. It was at that point they made that offer. The night before, I had received 1,000 emails. Within the first two weeks I received 10,000 emails. But on that first day when I received 1,000 emails, many of them were from people saying, "Congratulations, you're doing something great for customer service. Don't take the compensation that's coming, because you are doing something good for customers everywhere with your videos." I was kind of aware of that. The time it took them to make that offer of $1,200 and $1,200, I literally probably got 20 emails from people saying, "Please don't take it." It wasn't my intention to take it, and I was being supported from people around the world saying, "Please don't." So, it had become, not so much a cause, but something good for consumers.

Kenny: In thinking about that, it just came to me: if you had taken some kind of compensation, or if you showed that you might consider, they probably would have upped the offer and there would have been a negotiation. But you said you wouldn't take it. If you had taken it, it probably would have disappointed thousands, maybe millions of people. It may have really gone backward for you. I wonder if it would have backfired in the sense that your audience would have thought that maybe you were just in it for the money in the first place. That kind of ruins it. Maybe you wouldn't be where you are today with your success. You've always had good music, and I did read in the book about how you were pretty popular already. But now with your speaking and all that, if you would have taken compensation, there probably would have been a clause in the contract that said you can't speak about it anymore. I'm personally glad you didn't take it, and I hope that it has panned out for you.

Dave: It really has, but there was really never any plan to any of this. People have asked what my social media strategy was. It turned out that I had the video for a week and I had no idea what to do, so I just posted it at 11:30 pm on July 6, and four days later I had a million hits, and people started asking if I wanted to become a speaker. Somebody said, "You should write a book," and I got a book deal and all these things. Where I am today was totally not by design, it was by one door presenting itself and walking through. When I had the opportunity to accept compensation, I didn't, just for the reasons of what you outlined. I had friends who volunteered their time and energy and talent to make this first video and the other two that would follow. It didn't seem to me that if they had donated all of their time that I should take a payout. That was at the forefront of my mind as well.

Kenny: In your book there's a great quote, "We showed that any company's brand is nothing more than the sum of the stories being told about it." Dave, please expand upon that.

Dave: I didn't invent that saying; I heard it in different places from different people. It really explains what social media is about today. This idea that your brand today is different than it was before is so true. In the past, your brand was your logo. You controlled all the messaging around it if you paid enough advertising. People would definitely say what you wanted them to say about your brand. But now — in the age of social media — people have the ability to communicate with people all over the world and not support the one voice coming from the company if it doesn't ring true. We can't be brainwashed anymore.

If companies today want to have a strong and well-supported brand, the only way to do that is to engage with their customers and not dominate a conversation. You can try to lead it as a brand owner, but it's really a co-created experience today. The company owners who realize that are the ones who are actually making profit on it. There are many companies in the world that don't understand that there's profit in this co-created mentality. A lot of brand representatives actually fear social media, and they fear the idea that their customers might be telling them what to do — when at the end of the day, the customer has always been telling them what to do by whether they buy their products or not. So why not benefit and listen to what your customers have to say? By doing that, one thing that you get as a benefit is that many brands are getting innovations to their products that their own R & D departments haven't thought of yet, by nature of opening doors and letting good ideas come in from wherever.

Kenny: The author of *Socialnomics*, Erik Qualman, said that social media is going to take place around your business, and about your business, whether you like it or not. It's just a matter of whether you want to participate in the conversation. I think you hit on that in a different way there.

Dave: It's so true, and I've said that. I try and bring that out in my own presentations — that if you fear social media and choose not to engage because of that fear, you let that guide your decision on what you're going to do about it. That's your decision. You might be able to sustain your business for a while, but at the end of the day you can expect your competition will be embracing social media. You always have to go where your customers are, and today they're using social media. If you're not engaged, you're not there, and your customers will be dealing more with your competition.

Kenny: But if you're not listening, you won't even know. Dave, I advise my clients and teach my readers that you want to avoid looking like a commodity; you want to stand out from the competition. One way to do that is to inject personality into your business, and your marketing, and your story. In your book you talk about the race to the bottom, and how many businesses look to lower their prices as the only way to stand out. You go on to write, "Customers don't just choose what you make, they are buying the maker and the story behind the company that developed the product." Would you expand on that, Dave?

Dave: I think it occurred to me — and anybody can see this when you go shopping — sometimes stores are slashing prices to compete, and hopefully gain loyalty. But the race to the bottom doesn't ensure loyalty. All it does is ensure that you're going to keep dropping your price until your competition can't follow you anymore. But there are plenty of companies out there that don't engage in that, but they have loyal customers — usually because of the customer service that they offer and how they stand behind their products, with things like return policies, or even how they are treated.

If customers walk through the door and they get a smile and eye contact, and not just someone who is paid a minimum wage to stand there and do those things, but employees who actually look them in the eye and they care about what the customer is doing. They ask if they can help you, and if you say, "Yes, you can," they actually do help you. Those are the types of things that reward companies with loyalty.

Telling your story is so important. The power of story has never been more important in business today, because that's what stands out. In my own case, a great example is that I received an email from someone that started, "Mr. Carroll, I hate country music." I was convinced that it was going to be a damning email about "United Breaks Guitars," because it's definitely a country song. What it went on to say was, "But I appreciate what you did, I like your story, I like how you did it, and I'm going to go buy everything that you have for sale on your website, sight unseen." He hadn't even heard the songs. He bought $300 worth of products, a bunch of different CDs, a couple of t-shirts, and that sort of thing. Now, if I had tried to sell him the product, in this case, "United Breaks Guitars," I would have lost 99 cents, because he doesn't like country music. But because he bought my story, and he liked the way that I ran my business, and the integrity of the story, he bought everything I had. That's the difference. That's how you stand out in a busy environment today, whether it's social media or in regular business. How do you stand out? By sharing your story — who you are, not what you sell.

Kenny: Yes, that's a great story. I love country music, and one of the reasons I love it, I think is the same reason a lot of other people love it; there's an emotional attachment to country music by its biggest fans, and I believe that's primarily because of storytelling. Everyone likes a good story whether you're a country music fan or not. Now you just take that to your marketing and your communications — I think that can only be a good thing. Do you agree?

Dave: I do for sure, yes. I couldn't agree more.

Kenny: Consumer sites such as Gripevine exist because businesses fail to listen to their customers and brush some of them off as statistically insignificant, which you mentioned in your book. Gripevine will amplify the voice and reach of the unhappy customer. Obviously, businesses should do the right thing; they should offer great customer service and listen to their customers. But with regards to sites like Gripevine, what should businesses be doing?

Dave: Well, Gripevine is a company that I co-founded with Richard Hugh. We did it because of all those thousands of emails from people saying, "I wish I had a voice," "If I could sing I would do this," or, "I wish that I had an amplified voice." That was my motivation of getting involved—to help amplify the voice of consumers. This was also a good thing for companies. This comes back to what I said earlier about companies seeing social media either as the devil or as potential profit. Gripevine is potential profit for companies because it not only allows a place where consumers go to complain, it also makes one central complaining space. On Gripevine we ask people to be civil, no profanity is allowed, and most of all, consumers are asked to declare a solution if they're going to post a gripe. When we take your gripe and send it to a company, they get the whole story of what happened from someone who's civil and wants a solution, and they know what the solution will be. Sometimes a simple apology is all that's necessary. Other times, the customer might want a portion of their money back, or a full refund, or an exchange. That's really helpful to companies that are going into this age of social media where they have the same amount of stuff they have to do during the day, but now they have this social media dimension to handle as well.

Gripevine also offers companies the potential to be notified in real time when people are having problems with a product, so that they don't find out a week later somewhere else online when there are a million hits. Companies find out on the first day. We give them the opportunity to communicate offline with consumers because no company wants to have a public fight in an open forum. We ensure some level of privacy between the company and the consumer. Companies can do themselves a favor with things like Gripevine by engaging, and by taking the opportunities that companies like ours offer them, because more and more people are going to be using their electronic devices. There are more devices than there are people in the world now, and people are not only using social media more, but they are complaining more because it's so easy to complain. It's not labor intensive anymore. So the number of complaints around the world is going to go up exponentially, and how do companies deal with that? Well, companies like Gripevine have a dashboard that can handle that influx for them, and make it efficient and easy for them to communicate and make sure no customer gets lost.

Kenny: I recommend people — businesses and consumers — check Gripevine out. As a consumer, I already knew about some of these types of sites and I've also watched this sort of thing for my clients. I've come across a lot more of these complaint-type sites, and Gripevine is a little bit different. I'll tell you what I think, and you can correct me, or agree, but I've come across a lot more of these sites in doing research for my own book, which is around this topic, and also why I really wanted to interview you. Gripevine seems to be more of a solution site. A lot of the other ones I've seen are really just a place to go complain and fight the power, the evil empire. But Gripevine is, "No, let's get a solution." I love what you just said, "to post a gripe, you have to say what you want the solution to be." We're not here to just listen to you whine and complain. Tell us what's wrong, and let's find a solution. The business actually has a fair chance to get it solved without it hurting their business. That's what I'm getting out of it. Dave, would you say I'm on the right track there?

Dave: Very much so. I sort of started off today's interview by saying that I don't see "How to Break Guitars" as a story about confrontation. Depending on who you look to ask that question, you may get a different answer. But for me, on the surface I guess it looks that way, but if you go a little bit below that, I don't see it that way at all. Brand-bashing might make you feel a little better. I really don't think it does, it only maybe fires you up. It keeps you in that state of anger and frustration if you keep doing that. You might have people who come behind you and say, "I support you," but they're not the ones that are going to be giving you a refund. Having that attitude creates two sides, and two sides is not the way to find a solution. A resolution happens when two sides come together to find one solution. That's what we try to do at Gripevine. By having that sort of resolution-based idea, that invites companies to engage rather than try to bully them to engage; you're going to get more companies who are going to come to the table. When they do that, they don't get the sense that their brand and their image are being tarnished just by speaking to this person who's really angry. They'll be more inclined to reach a resolution, and we're all better off for it.

Kenny: Dave, one more thing I want to say, and it's more of a statement. If you have a comment about it I'd love to hear it. I think you've inspired everyday consumers and people to know that they have a voice, and they can do something about it. Most people would agree with that, but I think you've also inspired businesses to realize that every customer matters. I agree with you on what you said in your book. There was a point in the book where you mentioned being statistically insignificant. You said that when you do a gig, or you're recording a song, that you want it to be good 100 percent of the time. That's always the goal, but it's not always the reality. That's what you shoot for. And when businesses don't do that, they just open themselves up to a lot of problems. I think going for less is a horrible way for businesses to look at it, so I appreciate that you are bringing that understanding to them.

Many years ago, I was in the service business — in the restaurant business — and I looked at it as every customer mattered, not just what I made at the end of the day. For that customer, that may be an important experience of their life: they came to Vegas for the first time or last time, or their honeymoon. If you give them a bad experience, they're going to remember that forever. Whether it matters in your wallet or not, regardless — every customer matters. I guess there's not really a question there, but Dave, I think you've inspired both consumers and businesses. I appreciate that.

Dave: Thank you. What I noticed, and I didn't even really realize it until I started writing the book and looking deeper and deeper into what all of this meant, that my biggest take-away is that you and I and everybody in the world have a fundamental connection with one another. We pay lip service to that phrase that we are all connected, but I really do believe it on a fundamental level. For too long I think company owners have misunderstood where their business starts and ends, and what they're responsible for and where that ends as well. There is responsibility for customers as well. If we all see that we are all connected as part of this eco-system of commerce where there are consumers, and there are people who supply the products and services, and the ones who make those products and services, and the ones who manage — if everybody realizes it's all one eco-system, that changes everything. Then you wind up with companies who adopt this culture, they're the ones who try to get it right 100 percent of the time. They are massively different than the ones who only try for 95 percent of the time. The ones who shoot for 100 percent don't have annual general meetings where they say, "Congratulations, only 5 percent of our customers had a horrible experience." They're the ones that when they hear about a problem with a customer, it bothers them so much that not only they, but other people within the organization are scrambling at the same time to make it right for the right reasons. Customers who are engaging with a company from both examples. It's a powerful feeling that you get. It's something that, like you say, people don't forget.

Kenny: There is one last thing. Are you a movie buff? Do you watch a lot of movies?

Dave: Love movies.

Kenny: Did you see the movie *The Guardian* with Kevin Costner and Ashton Kutcher? He's a Coast Guard diver?

Dave: Yes, yes I did.

Kenny: There's a scene there, and it kind of reminds me of what you just said. It has to do with that 95, or shooting for 100 percent. There's a scene where Ashton Kutcher, his mentor is Kevin Costner — I don't remember their names in the movie, so I'll use their real names. Ashton Kutcher wants to know the number of people Kevin Costner has saved. That's the big thing. He says, "So, what's your number?" and Kevin Costner says something like 36, and Ashton Kutcher says, "Oh, that's a decent number. I thought it would have been higher, you're the man." Kevin Costner says, "That's how many I've lost." Ashton Kutcher was focused on how many he had saved. It reminds me of what you're talking about with the 95 and the five. You get where I'm coming with that?

Dave: Absolutely. A lot of my presentations, especially in customer service ones, often will end with a song that I wrote called, "Everyday Heroes" which has to do with First Responders. The reason I end my presentation with that is because the essence of the entire First Responder community is that there's this massive amount of technology that goes into building the 911 system, but the whole 911 system actually rests on the integrity of the individuals who respond to those calls. They are human beings who say, "I've got a certain skill, and if you call 911, I will come and give you — a perfect stranger — help, no matter where you are, maybe at the risk of losing my own life because I said that I would." And I like in that situation, a promise is enough.

I tie it into the presentation by saying that in customer service too many times companies have policies and regulations that they hide behind. They say, "We would like to help you. Yes, everything sounds right, but our policy is…"

and then they finish the sentence. Sometimes just the promise alone, "I want you to be satisfied," is all that the company should care about, and they should do everything they can to make it better. That would be profit for the company, and customers would be so loyal in this day where there are so many other options.

Kenny: I agree with that. Well, thank you for your time today Dave. I really appreciate it. I think you shared some great value. Please share what you're doing now, anything new, how business is, and how consumers can learn more about it.

Dave: If you want to come to my website, it's DaveCarrollMusic.com. You can see the main things that I'm doing right now, which is my book, music, and speaking. Those are the things I'm up to; I've been speaking all over the world, I like traveling, and love the differences in the audiences that I'm speaking to. Most of all, I love the fact that, as they say, the essence of my story cuts through culture and geography and language all over the world. It's got a universal truth to it, and I love rediscovering that every time.

Kenny: That is fabulous. Everybody check that out. Dave, I appreciate it. Thanks for the interview, and please keep me informed about that musical.

Dave: I will for sure Kenny, thanks a lot. I look forward to reading your book.

Kenny: Alright, I'll send you a copy. Thanks Dave.

Dave: Take care.

To protect yourself from customer complaints that go public, **KennyTalks.com** has resources for you.

Your call is important to us; please take a nap while you wait

A Comcast technician in the Washington, D.C., area had to call Comcast's help line in order to fix an Internet connection issue for a customer. The technician waited so long on the phone for customer service, that he eventually fell asleep on customer Brian Finkelstein's couch. The customer filmed the incident, added humorous text slides taking jabs at Comcast, and posted it online. The clip was picked up by a technology blog Gizmodo and was also shown on Keith Olbermann's program *Countdown* on MSNBC. Not surprisingly, this led to hundreds of thousands of views of the video in a short period of time.[45]

Stories like this leads to so much frustration and anger that unhappy customers create entire websites dedicated to bashing one company, such as ComcastMustDie.com.

Customers wield tremendous power with heavy artillery

When I was a kid there was a show called *Fight Back! With David Horowitz*. It ran from 1976-1992 and researched claims made by companies about the quality of their products. The show's focus wasn't to expose companies with poor customer service — its primary function was to alert consumers about fraudulent product promises.

Nowadays, a customer service show is not needed because consumers have the ability to create their own show on YouTube or their own news article on a blog or on Facebook or other types of social media platforms. Today, your customers have an arsenal of missiles to launch at your business when you make a mistake. It used to be that an unhappy customer would cost you one sale and possibly a few others through word of mouth. This is no longer the case. Now your customers have heavy artillery that they can and will use to launch an all-out assault against your business.

Your customers may not have the far-reaching voice of Dave Carroll and the ability to make a music video, but they wield a lot of power when upset, irritated, wronged, or frustrated. The United Airlines and Comcast examples are extreme stories. I share them because they *can* happen to you. It is more likely than not that customers will take advantage of one of many social platforms and review sites designed for talking about their experiences.

Platforms with the most impact

A 2013 Nielson study revealed the #3 most trusted form of advertising was *Consumer opinions posted online*. Online reviews fit into this category.[46]

If someone complains on their Facebook page or Twitter feed, a few people see it. Some of them may or may not be your potential customers.

If a customer complains on *your* Facebook page, a few of your customers will see it and you can respond with a regular dialogue.

Possibly the most impactful are online reviews. Those little orange stars show up right next to your business name and address whether you like it or not. It is like graffiti on the side of your building or across the front of your website.

When someone does a generic Google search for your category of business, a list of businesses appear on the screen, all with online reviews and the review rating. When a potential customer does a brand search specifically looking for your type of business, your online reviews stand out quite obviously on the screen. Even if the person searches specifically for your business because they were referred to you or they saw your commercial, other customer experiences in the form of reviews are now right there in front of them. They can't help but look.

While doing research for this book, I did a Google search for *Complain about a company online*. There were 56.8 million results. I don't know if there are over 56 million places to complain about a business but there are many; all of the local directories provide an avenue for customers to write an online review.

In the last two years, Google made five major changes that make online reviews more important.

Nearly 5,000 consumers were contacted for the 2015 Local Consumer Review Survey conducted by BrightLocal. The survey revealed the following:

- *92% of consumers now read online reviews (vs. 88% in 2014)*
- *40% of consumers form an opinion by reading just 1-3 reviews (vs. 29% in 2014)*
- *Star rating is #1 factor used by consumers to judge a business*
- *44% say a review must be written within one month to be relevant*

- *Only 13% of consumers consider using a business that has a 1 or 2-star rating*
- *68% say positive reviews make them trust a local business more (vs. 72% in 2014)[47]*

Online reviews are everywhere

Entire companies have been birthed and thrived at some point by focusing on displaying customer reviews online. Other online giants such as Google and Facebook have made it a big part of their Internet platforms.

Government agencies have even jumped in on the action. The Consumer Financial Protection Bureau (CFPB) included a message along with IRS tax returns asking customers, *Do you have a complaint about financial products and services? Visit consumerfinance.gov/complaint or call...*

The CFPB then posted complaints publicly on their website for the entire world to see.

Your existing happy customers read your reviews too

Every business needs a steady supply of new customers coming in, but even if you were silly enough to think that you only need the customers you already have, there is still a problem. Your existing customers can read your questionable reviews and may be turned away.

One of my clients, Frank, hired us to conduct a survey campaign to collect data from his customers. We were giving away a golf outing and dinner at a restaurant. He told me what restaurant he wanted to use — one that he frequented. Frank called me a few hours after our meeting while I was writing the advertising copy for his campaign. He wanted to switch restaurants. I asked why. He said that the restaurant recently had some negative online reviews.

Frank may have been concerned that the service had changed for the worse. Or if the restaurant was still great, Frank may have been concerned that a few recent, poor reviews could reflect badly on him if he gave his own valuable customers a gift certificate to the place.

Getting someone to refer business to you is harder than getting the same customer to buy from you again. Nobody wants to have a friend call and say, "That place you referred me to — STINKS!"

In the first chapter I shared my story about choosing another doctor after reading his negative online reviews. My initial experience with the doctor in the hospital was good and I left anyway.

What does all this mean? In part, it means that you can't advertise around your online reviews. They either help or hurt all of your advertising, because most of the ads you use send people straight to the Internet to read what others say about you.

Your online reviews matter. They have become more important each year over the last several years. Google and others post reviews about your business which makes reviews more important, but it's actually the consumer who influences companies such as Google — and that's why reviews are posted in the first place. Some customers want to know what other people say about your business before they spend any of their time and money on you.

CHAPTER 9

Turning Volunteers into Super Soldiers

The most powerful marketing team ever assembled — your customers.

Nothing you say about your business via marketing/advertising has near as much impact as what your customers say about you.

This chapter will cover two main topics:

1. How to keep your customers from publicly speaking negatively about you

2. How to turn your customers into super soldiers who rally around your business

Because the example of a $180 million mistake is fresh in your mind, let's have a look at how to keep your customers from publicly bashing your business.

First, be awesome!

I wish I could move on from that and let that be enough, but it's tough to be awesome all of the time; and you are not totally in control of all of your team. The bigger your business, the less direct control you have.

Some tips about how to be awesome so your customers stay happy and loyal:

- Hire the right people
- Great boot camp training
- Excellent ongoing training
- Interesting place to work
- Terrific product and services

Despite your best effort, there is a customer who is not happy. Your attempts to rectify the situation after the fact could keep them from machine gun firing disgruntled comments to everyone they know and/or posting negative comments online.

You read earlier about handling mistakes quickly. But wait! There's more!

Customers can have hair-trigger emotional reactions. For example, a server brings a cold steak to the booth and before the customer even leaves the restaurant, he's left a negative review online along with a small tip on the table.

As previously mentioned, using a complaint management and feedback system to regularly hear from your customers is something you should seriously consider. Establish a direct line of communication from customers to ownership. Make it easy for customers to offer feedback, glowing or not. This does not mean 20-question surveys. Right after or during the final process of the sale is the best time to request customer feedback. Do not give them time to stew over something that made them unhappy or publicly spread something negative without first giving you a chance to fix it. You also don't want to lose the opportunity to get a testimonial while they are at their happiest point, usually at the point of sale.

Remember also that your feedback system should be sabotage-proof from employees. Although some employees may be wary about it, make sure they understand that the system is meant to keep small issues from becoming big issues.

Don't make the mistake of thinking that you don't need a feedback system because your customers will let you know when they are unhappy. For every customer who bothers to complain, 26 others remain silent.[48]

A good feedback system will also help you spread positive feedback and earn positive online reviews. This becomes a valuable marketing asset; it is a treasure house for you to open whenever you launch a new campaign. You can tap into this vault to display positive customer comments in your advertising copy and increase conversion rates.

Imagine a system that allows your customers to leave feedback; it segments them into happy versus unhappy customers. This system directs those unhappy consumers directly to a message from you that states, "Whenever I get feedback like yours I like to find out why, and to see what we can do to fix the problem. Please share as much as possible." This system also directs happy buyers to a message that says, "Thanks! Glad you had a great experience.

The great news is that you don't have to imagine this system just described to you — because it exists. **Go to KennyTalks.com for feedback systems, tips and tools.**

Humanize your business — helps avoid negative but also boosts positive comments

Add personality to your enterprise and give a "face to the business." Communicate with your customers at times other than when you ask for their money. When your customer thinks of you as a human/person instead of a faceless entity, they will cut you some slack when things don't go perfectly, and they are more likely to develop a bond and loyalty to your business.

A few tactical maneuvers to humanize your business:

- *Newsletters* — There is an entire chapter dedicated to this. Read it again.

- *Videos* — On your website, in your emails, or in your email newsletters. Your face, your voice, your mannerisms — all lead to you looking more like a human and less like a logo.

- *Thank you notes* — Delivered thank-you notes printed on paper. It means more to the recipient. Don't just believe me — try sending an eCard to Grandma for Christmas.

- *Surprises* — A surprise note, gift, or communication. "Just calling to say, 'Hi.' Did your son get that football scholarship?"

- *Events* — Customer appreciation parties. Have them.

Connect and/or like your customer?

Customers will buy from you again and refer business based not only on how they feel about you, but also based on how you feel about them. As mentioned in an earlier chapter, an actor making $10 million dollars in a movie delivers a poor acting performance once in a while. If a "professional" actor practices their entire life, gets paid $10 million and still does a poor job of being convincing, not even you can pretend to like your customers and be convincing.

> "I do not like that man. I must get to know him better." ~Abraham Lincoln

Get to know more about your customers. Find out their story. This will humanize them to *you*. It will help get you out of the habit of thinking about them only as a customer rather than a human who happens to give you money in exchange for your services. Sometimes customers are a pain; they are human.

I've had clients who have had successful businesses handed down to them from family. They've always had money and they have always had a job or career. That is nothing to feel bad about. Nobody would turn that chance away if given the opportunity. However, it does mean that they may have a hard time relating to their customers.

When writing copy for a client, I want to get into the heads of their customers and relate to them as best I can.

I read what they read, watch what they watch, and try to experience life the way they experience it. I will at least try to understand and relate to them.

Take an interest in your customer. You will remember things about them if you are truly interested — but don't leave it up to memory. Use a CRM tool. Remembering things about customers makes them feel special. "You remembered that?" they'll say. Don't respond to that question with, "Yes, we use a CRM — Customer Relationship Management Tool." You just took away their moment of feeling special to you. That's like telling a woman she looks pretty and fit, and when she says, "Really?" you respond with, "Well it must be the dress."

Go through your own buying process

Step outside of your own head for a moment. Have an out-of-body experience and pretend to be one of your customers. Forget about your story of how you struggled to get where you are today. Forget that you are an honest person. Forget that you have a great team of people working for you and the best product and service, blah, blah, blah. Your potential customer and some of your existing customers don't know about any of that. All they know is their experience with you and past experiences with other companies that they think are just like you.

For example, cite an instance of something that seems obvious to you but might not be to your customer. The word "Finance" on your website may not jump out at your customer, but "Apply for Financing" might. Your customer doesn't know that he or she should go to the plumbing section of the home improvement store to get pipes for landscaping. They thought it would be in the landscaping section. However, this deduction seems obvious to you because you are in the business. You do it every day. Your customer may deal with your business once a month or once a year.

Mark Cuban is the star of Shark Tank and owner of the Dallas Mavericks. In his book, *How to Win at The Sport of Business*, he writes, "You have to re-earn your customers business every day...I personally think the only way you can connect to your customers is to put yourself in their shoes."

Cuban goes on to explain that he goes to Mavericks games, stands in line, buys his ticket and his drink, and experiences a game in the same way that a fan does.

Cuban is one of the wealthiest entrepreneurs in the world. If he can go through the buying and service process of his businesses, so can you.

Have you experienced this?

"Press 1 for English."

"Press 2 for sales."

"Press 3 for department A."

"Press 4 for department B."

"Press 5 for department C."

"Press 6 for department D."

"Press 7 if you are irritated by now."

"Press 8 if you know your call is **not** that important to us."

"Press 9 for customer service."

"Press 17 if you didn't hear a number for your need."

Oh wait there is not a 17 on my phone!

"That's right customer. There is no number for your specific need. Good luck!"

Uuuuuuurrrrrrggg!

How about I just hang-up and call your competitor? How about that?

I've tried hitting "0" as soon as I hear the auto-attendant. Now these wise guys have recorded a message that says, "I understand you want to speak to a customer service rep but I need to know why you are calling."

And the process starts over.

Admit it. You have been through this process before. How do you feel when you finally get someone on the phone? After all that rigmarole, if something goes even remotely less than perfect, how do you feel about your overall experience?

Right now you may be thinking, *We don't have an auto-attendant. A human answers our phone.* That's not the point.

The point is that there is more than likely something somewhere in your business where something does not go as it should, or that the customer can't stand, and it makes them angry. Their experience starts from a hole and makes it an uphill battle from the beginning.

Eighty percent of companies say they deliver "superior" customer service

Only 8 percent of people think these same companies deliver "superior" customer service[49]

Don't leave it up to chance. Do your business a favor and experience your company's *complete* process for yourself.

Communication malpractice

Really listen to your customers' testimonials, complaints, and recommendations. Stephen Covey wrote in his best-selling book, *The Seven Habits of Highly Effective People,* "Seek first to understand, then to be understood." In Habit 5, Covey explains that most people do not listen with intent to understand; they listen with intent to reply. They are already preparing their response while the other person is still talking. He gives an example of a doctor who prescribes something for a patient before diagnosing that patient. That is malpractice. Don't commit communication malpractice on your customers.

Create incredible experiences

"Whatever you do, do it well. Do it so well that when people see you do it they will want to come back and see you do it again and they will want to bring others and show them how well you do what you do." ~Walt Disney

People will pay up to three times as much for a product or experience that they find "intensely captivating."[50]

Garth Brooks won Entertainer of the Year six times from 1990-1998. During interviews, he regularly said that he didn't have the best voice and he wasn't the best-looking, but he worked hard to make sure that everyone had a great experience.

Joshie the Giraffe

Think about unique ideas that will provide an experience for your customers that they can't keep to themselves. Some may go viral. For example, the story of Joshie the Giraffe and the Ritz-Carlton:

Chris Hurn's family stayed at the Ritz-Carlton on Amelia Island in Florida. When they returned home from their holiday they realized that they had forgotten Joshie the Giraffe, Chris's young son's best friend.

After Chris called the hotel to see if they could locate the toy, he explained to his son that Joshie was having a little extra holiday, and that he was fine.

That evening someone from the Ritz-Carlton called to say that they had found Joshie in the laundry room and that he had been handed over to the Loss Prevention Team. Chris told them his little white lie about Joshie's extra holiday and wondered if they would mind taking a picture of Joshie on a chair by the pool to "prove" it!

The team at the Ritz-Carlton went above and beyond their call to duty. A few days later, a package arrived with a few Ritz-Carlton branded goodies and a binder that documented Joshie's adventures. They took pictures of Joshie the Giraffe sunbathing by the pool wearing sunglasses, meeting with other "furry friends," having a massage at the spa, and driving down to the beach in a golf cart. There was even a picture of Joshie working at security cameras making sure that other things didn't get lost.[51]

In the spirit of Henry Ford — how can you take this idea and make it work for your business?

Trust

Much of what has been written about in this chapter is to keep and earn your customers' trust. People all over the world have experienced poor service, outright lies and thievery. They have read about high-profile scandals and disgusting experiences. Their perceptions of your business are already slanted by what they have heard about others and by past disappointing experiences.

Trust is critical. Once you have it you must keep it.

People pay extra for trust. Remember the story of my dad hanging Christmas lights for wealthy clients?

In Stephen M.R. Covey's book, *Smart Trust*, he shares the five actions of Smart Trust:

1. Choose to believe in trust

2. Start with ourselves

3. Declare our intent and assume positive intent in others

4. Do what we say we are going to do

5. We can lead in extending smart trust to others

Creating super fans

Implementing most of what you have read so far in this chapter may lead you to developing marketing soldiers. If you are still pushing for more, you may look to what Harley Davidson or Hard Rock Café did in years past.

Harley "riders" get tattoos on their arms and other places I can't mention in this PG-rated book. They wear the gear and go to huge events — all to celebrate their membership in the cool kids club. They go to brand-sponsored and promoted events, and they create their own events. Harley has earned a strong following because they have created a feeling of belonging. Harley "riders" are part of a community known as the "Harley family."

The Hard Rock Café has made millions of dollars worldwide selling food, drinks, and promotional items such as t-shirts and guitar pins. In the 1990s, the Las Vegas location earned about $21 million per year with over 55 percent of that revenue coming from t-shirts and other promotional merchandise. Customers went in for a $20 lunch and left with $60 worth of merchandise. Some patrons skipped eating and went straight to the merchandise area to purchase a bag full of stuff for themselves or friends who didn't make the vacation.

How would you like to have your company name or logo tattooed on your customers' bodies? How about having your customers parade around town like a human billboard for your company? Think about that for a moment; your company being promoted in ink on chests, backs, and even on top of bald heads. Not only that, your customers gladly pay you for the privilege!

Both Harley Davidson and Hard Rock Café entrepreneurs have developed a deep connection with their customers. The connection does not come from having the lowest prices or from being just like everyone else. Both companies provide an experience different from that of their competitors. There are other motorcycles, but not with the loud, unique pop-pop...pop-pop...pop-pop as someone rides by.

There are plenty of restaurants that serve a good hamburger and French fries — but not with the atmosphere of rock-n-roll playing while looking at millions of dollars of rock-n-roll memorabilia. There are not many restaurants that people want to prove they have visited by buying a t-shirt or hat. The Hard Rock Café provides a cool place to have an experience instead of just eating a burger and fries.

Quick tips to grow your marketing soldier base:

- Be unique. No one will want to wear your gear around town or battle for your brand if their friends can purchase the same thing elsewhere.

- Provide an incredible experience — not just a product or service.

- Make your customers feel like they belong to something — a community.

- Make your customers feel cool from having purchased from you.

- Don't try to be the "lowest price-loser," or the previous four won't be possible.

Boot camp for customers

Your customers probably won't run 10 miles and tread water in ice cold temperatures at customer boot camp, but you can teach them how to refer business. To erase confusion, let's start with "how to refer:"

How to refer should include:

- *Specificity* — Asking your customers to tell others to check out your website is not specific enough. It's better for them to say to their friends, "Go to their website and download the super-duper checklist."

- *Humanize* — There's that word again. When possible, have your customers refer to a person and not the business. Businesses are faceless. It's more comfortable for a potential customer when they are referred to a person.

- *What NOT to do* — Every business category has a negative perception, and it's wise not to focus on it. It's better if a patient describes how much better they feel after visiting a chiropractor versus all of the cracks and pops they experienced from having their necks and spines aligned.

- *Watch your words* — Watching your words will influence your customers to watch their own words. It sounds better if your customers speak to their friends and refers to your business as their favorite business that will "help you," versus "sell to you." A restaurant should refer to patrons as "guests," not "customers." A team of people who sell should refer to themselves as "advisors," not "salespeople."

How to get customers to enroll in boot camp

Customers may not show up in camouflage, but they may consume the information that you give to them. Create a short, fun booklet to hand out after their happy experience. Acknowledge that your customer may know others who are interested in your goods and services. Explain how you would like to be introduced to people that they know.

Include tips for referring others to your business in your newsletter that goes out to your customers regularly (see Chapter 3).

Host "customer and friends" events where your customers come with their friends for free sandwiches and drinks — then your customers don't have to know how to refer.

It's okay to simply ask for referrals. For example: *By now, you have some ideas to grow your business after having read this book. You probably know a business owner or someone who runs an organization and would benefit greatly from this book. Do them a favor — and me a favor — and send them an email with a link to purchase my book. Better yet, surprise them with a gift and buy a copy for them.* See how easy that is to ask?

Give your customers tools so that they can refer. They may not remember the boot camp lesson you gave them about how you like to be introduced. Give them tools for doing so. You can bet that my best clients will get two copies of this book — one for them to read and one to give to a business owner friend. If you are not an author, create something that would be valuable to a potential customer that your existing customer can give to a friend. It could be a friend-coupon or something similar.

Referral programs

"The mercenaries will always beat the draftees, but the volunteers will crush them both." ~Chuck Noll

When it comes to your customers, your goal should be to turn them into volunteer soldiers who go to battle for you because they want to, not because they were paid to. I am not suggesting that a monetary referral does not work, but consider this:

If you have terrible service and a terrible product but you have the world's highest-paying referral program, how many referrals can you expect? Not many. How much repeat business can you expect? Not much.

On the other hand, many companies have outstanding service and/or products and people refer friends and family to them and talk about them in a positive way, all the time. Repeat purchases for that company are the norm.

Get best results recruiting super soldiers

Attract ideal customers. Laser-targeting leads to leads to higher conversions, better experiences, better reviews, word-of-mouth referrals, and referrals that are an ideal fit. Attracting a vegetarian to your steakhouse will make money for you today, but won't lead to many repeat purchases. The measly three vegetarian items on the menu will not excite the vegetarian enough to want to come back often. You've probably heard the phrase, "Birds of a feather flock together." Vegetarians have vegetarian friends. Don't expect many referrals from meat-free diners at your steakhouse.

Identify your ideal customer target by looking closely at your current customers. Discover their similarities and figure out how to advertise to others with these similarities. It may not be obvious at a glance. That next step may require some serious reconnaissance and intelligence research.

CHAPTER 10

CIA - Reconnaissance

The CIA's primary mission is to collect, analyze, evaluate, and disseminate foreign intelligence information. Their data is given to the President and senior US government policymakers to help them make decisions about national security.

There are several ways to collect information. Translating foreign newspaper and magazine articles, and radio and television broadcasts provides open-source intelligence. Satellites take pictures from space for imagery analysts to write reports about what they see; for example, how many airplanes are sitting at a foreign military base. Signals analysts decrypt coded messages sent by other countries. Operations officers recruit foreigners to give knowledge about their countries.

After the material is collected, intelligence analysts pull together relevant information from all available sources and assess the following: what is happening, why it is happening, what might occur next, and what it means for U.S. interests. The results of these analytic efforts are timely and objective assessments free of any political bias, which are provided to senior U.S. policymakers in the form of written reports and oral briefings. One of these reports is the President's Daily Brief (PDB), an Intelligence Community product which the U.S. president and other senior officials receive each day.[52]

Form your own CIA

Your company CIA needs to collect, analyze, evaluate, and disseminate market intelligence to help you make decisions regarding the success of your organization. This intelligence should include a hodgepodge of information for all aspects of your business.

A variety of methods to collect information is easily available if you understand its importance, take action, and collect it. Other information will need to be collected via a clandestine approach.

Depending upon the size of your organization, you may not need a President's Daily Brief — but your information-gathering and review should take place on a regular basis.

Eight important research principles:

1 - Research customers

For marketing purposes, identify your ideal customer target by looking closely at your current customers. Dig deeper to learn more about them in order to build a stronger bond. You will learn how to cater offers, messages, upgrades, and all communications to keep them moving forward. In a previous chapter I wrote about hosting customer appreciation parties. Imagine your intelligence gathering team finding out the main type of food or restaurant that your customers like. You could have your customer appreciation party catered by that restaurant. If you are already wisely sending out a newsletter to your customers, you can include information that you know will interest your customer. This creates connection.

You may think these small details are minor, but they may be the difference between your customer seriously considering your competitor's next coupon that arrived in their mailbox or throwing it in the trash.

2 - Research competitors

Much of the marketing and advertising your competitors use is easily accessible because they lack the stealth marketing that you have learned about in this book. You can see their television ads, hear their radio spots, look at their print ads, check out their websites, and view their ads on Google.

Researching your competitors will help you decide what to do along with what to avoid. When managing a client's Google Pay-Per-Click ads we make a list of relevant keywords and phrases that a potential customer may type into Google when searching for your product or service category. Then, acting as a potential customer, we do a Google search and look at the 10 or so ads that appear on the screen. We take a screenshot of those ads and put them on a Word document. We do the same thing for several other keywords. When we are finished, we look at ALL of the ads at the same time. We look for good ideas. Then we look for similarities in the advertisements — so that we can do the opposite. We want your advertisement to be different in every way possible.

Going through their buying process is a great way to get more in-depth knowledge about your competitors.

Alan Mulally, former CEO of Ford Motor Company, wanted to compare Ford to its competitors. He had fleet managers buy Camrys and other non-Ford vehicles. Mulally ordered his senior managers to drive Volkswagens and Hondas instead of their up-market Jaguars and Land Rovers in order to learn about the competition.

3 - Research non-direct competitors

Anyone who consumes your customers' time and attention or their money is a competitor. If a company outside of your category sells something to your target customer, it is a good idea to spy on them too. Look at their marketing. What resonating message are they conveying to your target market? With a few small tweaks you can most likely make it work for you. It is the same customer — just a different category.

4 - Research the market

Overall, what is happening in the marketplace? This information can be gleaned from industry trade journals, associations, and from attending conventions. In the same way that the CIA analyzes satellite pictures from space, you should take a broad view of the industry as a whole to identify and capitalize on marketplace trends.

5 - Researching new markets or areas of need

Go on a reconnaissance mission. If you are considering entering a new market or adding a product or service, go through the buying process of another company that offers whatever it is that you want to add. I have a client in the automotive business who wanted to start a car wash. I went to the busiest car wash I could find. I wasn't sure if they were successful but they looked like it. I paid and acted like a normal customer. I asked questions during the process and was able to get a plethora of details to share with my client. The manager told me how busy they were, how many cars they wash in a month, and when they are not busy and why.

A second type of reconnaissance mission is to call a company from outside of your area to get advice. Make sure the owner knows that you are not a competitor. Offer to pay for the information. Learning about the market prior to entering could save you a ton of money and headaches.

A third type of reconnaissance mission is to get consulting from a successful company in the category that you are researching. A variety of successful companies have created consulting or coaching programs to help other companies in their industry. If you need help finding one, go to **KennyTalks.com**. If you have already found one and want to tout their skills, please let me know by going to **KennyTalks.com** and clicking on *Industry Experts*.

I've already mentioned Zappos, a shoe and clothing company headed by Tony Hsieh. They are known for their customer service and culture. Training is offered through Zappos Insights.

Disney Institute is the professional development arm of The Walt Disney Company. They offer solutions for best practices, sound methodologies, and real-life business lessons to facilitate corporate culture change.

If you are highly successful and want to start a coaching or consulting program of your own, get our free, express checklist for *Starting a Coaching Program*, at **KennyTalks.com**

6 - Research outside of your industry

The biggest breakthrough ideas come from outside of your industry. Copying the competition in your category and making tweaks only allows for incremental improvements. It is *outside* of your industry that you find ideas to use that none of your competitors thought about.

In his 2002 book, *Customers for Life: How to Turn That One-Time Buyer Into a Lifetime Customer*, Carl Sewell said to "Borrow, borrow, borrow." Sewell transformed his Dallas Cadillac dealership into the second largest in America at one time. He borrowed Chuck E. Cheese's order-taking and notification system, floors from McDonald's, and grounds cleanliness from Disney. Japanese culture taught him about hospitality.

Researching outside of your industry is a standard I consider to be so important and impactful that it is one of the principles I teach in my training program, **Breakthrough Ideas and New Solutions**. Go to **KennyTalks.com** for more information.

7 - Study successful people and businesses

Libraries and bookstores everywhere are full of highly successful people who reveal their thought processes and secrets from the beginning of their hugely successful organization. Tap into that.

Study highly successful organizations today. If shares are publicly traded you can look at all of the numbers and get access to their shareholder letters; a variety of information may lead to your next great idea. I have made purchases and donations to many just to see what type of communication I receive afterward.

Studying and researching other successful, highly unusual or interesting companies may lead to unique solutions that you might have never thought about.

8 - When to research?

With the threat of the powerful communist Soviet Union and the Cold War looming in 1946, President Truman soon recognized the need for a centralized intelligence system — even in **peacetime**.[53]

Your CIA should collect information all the time. There is no peacetime. There will always be a competitor who battles for the time, attention, and money of your existing and prospective customers.

I find it useful to wear two sets of learning glasses when I research. Information gleaned is entered into my ideas and research files. When you watch a movie or a television show, enjoy the entertainment as part of the audience; but also wear your explorer glasses and wonder these things: *Why was the joke told at a specific moment? Why did a commercial air at a specific minute? Why did product placement happen at a specific time?*

A warning about information and intelligence

This chapter has been dedicated to gathering and analyzing information. I must end with this: at some point you have to make a decision and get started. Some of your best information from gathering and analysis will happen **WHILE** you are moving and implementing.

Don't suffer from the long-term effects of analysis paralysis.

CHAPTER 11

Becoming a Superpower

According to Wikipedia, "A superpower is a state with a dominant position in international relations and is characterized by its unparalleled ability to exert influence or project power on a global scale... a superpower is a nation or state that has mastered the seven dimensions of state power; geography, population, economy, resources, military, diplomacy and national identity."

If your company can earn a dominant position to exert influence or drive to power in your industry — you will have a major advantage. In order to be a superpower, you need to master several dimensions.

Go through this book again and make plans to dominate more than one area to get your superpower status.

In nearly every successful case, entrepreneurs worked to be #1 at something or many things to attain their company's superpower status. The top dog always has an advantage. In some cases, they made the rules and/or set trends and the direction of an entire industry.

Our society is heavily skewed toward being #1

People want to work with #1. They want to be around success. This is why a busy restaurant gets more interest than an empty restaurant. The nightclub with a line of customers outside attracts the eyes and interests of people driving by more than a club where nobody is standing outside.

Being #1 allows you to command premium pricing. Being #2, not so much.

According to more than one study of Search Engine rankings over the years, the #1 ranked website after a given search would get clicked on as much as numbers 2, 3, and 4 put together.

Ask 10 people if they can name the second President of the United States off the top of their heads.

Can you name the World Series or the Super Bowl runners-up from two years ago?

Still not convinced?

- Name the top place to purchase books online. Now name the second most popular.
- Name the top auction website. Now name the second most popular.

You can study the science and psychology behind the "being #1" phenomenon -- or you can just accept it and strive to be #1.

Maybe it's not about being #1 for you. Maybe would like to be a superpower without being #1. You may want to be the best superpower that you can possibly be.

Snowball effect

Imagine pushing a snowball up the steeper side of a mountain while the sun shines on that side. When you stop to rest, the snowball begins to melt. As you push the snowball up the sunlight-filled side of the mountain, pushing gets more difficult and the snowball slowly melts. You believe that you are getting near the top of the mountain, but you can't see the peak because it is covered in fog and clouds.

Most people stop pushing at this point.

Despite the struggle, you continue pushing the snowball and eventually get to the summit. From here you can roll the snowball downward. It is easier to roll now. A snowball rolling downhill picks up more snow as it goes, which causes it to be heavier and therefore, rolls faster. The surface area of the snowball also grows which makes it pick up more snow on its descending journey. The bigger and heavier the snowball gets, the faster it goes.

- *The snowball* = Your business
- *The mountain* = Challenges of achieving success
- *The sun* = Negatives thoughts and/or setbacks

During your struggle to get your business to the mountaintop, you try new marketing tactics that fail. As you improve your hiring and training process, employees leave. You lose customers while you improve your customer relations and service.

When you get to the pinnacle, you have put systems and processes in place that make everything function better. You continue to advertise, and your existing customers continue to buy from you. More happy customers means more word-of-mouth advertising and more positive online talk. Your advertising is more effective because you are seen as trustworthy and your conversion percentages increase. This all leads to more customers…and the snowball keeps growing.

How to become a Superpower

Use the ideas we've presented in this book that make the most sense for you. You can increase the value of a customer by using many of the ideas you have read about in this book. This allows you to outspend your competitor to acquire the same customer. You give yourself an economic advantage which essentially positions you at the top of the mountain.

Positioning

Position yourself with a better reputation by having an emotional connection with people who buy from you. If you have important expertise in your business, position yourself by becoming an author. There is a reason why "author" is in the word "authority." When you are an author, you are seen as the authority in your market. To simplify the process of becoming an author, go to www.BookByInterview.com. I did not use this process for writing this book, but I wish I had. It would have been easier.

Be unique

Have you ever wondered at what point military leaders figured out that marching in a straight line during battle was a poor strategy? Do something different — finally.

Don't be boring

Boredom kills businesses. When the economy struggles, guess which industry thrives? Entertainment. Offer entertainment value in your marketing or in your delivery of service. While delivering a keynote or a workshop speech, I try to look for opportunities to make an audience laugh. They want to learn, but they don't want to feel like they are in calculus class — even if they love math.

Use multiple forms of media

At any moment a specific media may be rendered useless by a governmental regulation, an algorithm change, or a change in the marketplace. Using multiple forms of media protects you and puts your business everywhere. It positions you like a successful company. Different forms of media can support each other in a creative, productive way. Successful marketing campaigns often begin with direct mail that drives prospects to a website. Once on the website, the prospective customer fills out a form and receives a follow-up email. That's three forms of media in use right there.

Implement everything right now

Lee Iacocca was asked during an interview what he did **first** to turn around Chrysler. He said, "First? We did everything at the same time."

Don't work on new marketing without fixing a customer service problem. Don't work solely on a customer service problem and wait to devise a new marketing campaign. In both instances there are customers who are buying from someone else **right now**. Those new customers who purchased their goods elsewhere will refer other buyers to your competitors (the snowball effect working against you.)

Implementing everything right now will likely require outside assistance. Make a list of your needs and what can be done in-house and then follow with a list of what requires the services of a consultant or coach.

Messy beds get men killed

You've probably heard that if a soldier's bed isn't so tightly made that a quarter bounces off of it during a barracks inspection, that soldier will be running miles or on latrine duty for a week. The idea is that if you can't even make your bed precisely, how can you be trusted to clean your gun? This also imparts discipline that everything matters — all of the time.

Former New York Mayor Rudolph Giuliani who is credited by many with cleaning up New York during his term, subscribes to the "Broken Windows" theory as originally put forth by professors James Q. Wilson and George L. Kelling in a piece in the *Atlantic Monthly* magazine in 1982.

Mayor Giuliani believes that you must pay attention to small things, otherwise they get out of control and become much worse; small problems should be dealt with at the earliest possible stage.[54]

The little things *do* matter in your business, and they must be dealt with at the earliest possible stage.

Think back to Chapter 7 with the example of an employee saying, "Hi" instead of, "Hello" which eventually leads to, "Whassup?" There are rules and training that you have put into place that if let go, will become something entirely different than what you originally intended. A small variance turns into a big problem later.

I've experienced this myself. I travelled to meet a client for two days of consulting in Texas. I boarded a plane and sat down in first class. I like the fact that in first class you get a comfortable seat, and food or drink right away if you choose. I was hungry and pulled out the food tray from beneath the armrest to get ready to order. Down inside the armrest was a plethora of old food. It was disgusting. My thought was, *If they can't take care of the parts of the plane that customers see, is the rest of the plane getting checked out and maintained?*

Get in the Command Center

Join a group of smart entrepreneurs and brainstorm together. One constant in Albert Einstein's life was spending time with Mastermind groups. The days spent with the Olympian Academy clique were perhaps the most joyous in Einstein's life. Decades later, tears welled in his eyes when he recalled the vibrant, audacious claims they made as they voraciously devoured the major scientific works of the day.[55]

Groups of like-minded people will stimulate your brain and lead to ideas you may not otherwise encounter. A good group will also hold each other accountable. That's what happens in Twenty Groups in the automotive industry.

Soldiers train in peacetime — so should you

Never stop consuming ideas and information. Subscribe to newsletters. Go to workshops, conferences, and conventions. Invest in training for your team and for yourself. Your next breakthrough idea may seem like it came out of nowhere, but you will have earned it because you are constantly filling your head with good intel.

Words kill — words give life

For good reason, there are books written entirely about how to use words in advertising and communications. The way in which words are used will either lead people to buy from you or make them head out the door. Words are influential. Watch and listen to politicians. Both Liberals and Conservatives are careful with their words. When referring to something they want you to support they use words that conjure up images in your head of fairies, pixie dust, and butterflies. When politicians want you to fight against something, they use words to make you feel anxious, uneasy, or even angry toward whatever it is that they refer to.

Words that you use in your sales letters, emails, commercials and other advertisements either influence people to learn more about you and buy from you — or they don't. Words matter.

A quick and simplified way to discover the true power of your words is to do a split-test of an advertisement. Send the same amount of postcards or other sales communication such as fliers to two groups of like-minded people, changing only one or two words. Look at the difference in responses. I've split-tested email subject lines for clients and for my own company's emails that have already had a pretty good open rate. By changing a few words, I increased the open rate of those emails by over 100 percent at times.

Make a list of weapons

You wouldn't arm your soldiers with BB guns. Use the best tools possible in every aspect of your business. The best military force in the world couldn't do diddly-squat without planes and tanks.

Lethal weapons only work if you take them out of the holster. Make a list of tools that are critical for your business as well as a list of tools that may work. I've consulted with business owners who have difficulty getting their employees to use their CRM. It only works if you use it. That doesn't mean to scrap it. Again — decide which tools are critical and which tools are only *chasing the next shiny object.*

For thousands of years humans have needed to leverage tools and weapons. Before he was King of Israel, David thwarted a military threat by leveraging a simple tool that allowed him to overcome the size and physical advantages of the Philistine giant Goliath. David didn't choose an expensive or elaborate tool. If he had tried to fight Goliath sword-to-sword or hand-to-hand he would have lost. David used the tools at hand — stones and a slingshot — that made sense for the situation and single-handedly defeated the enemy.

Soldiers and weapons without strategy

Using tools without strategy is similar to old military battles where soldiers lined up in a row, started marching toward each other and shooting. "Hold the line!" they shouted to each other. Then one day someone likely said,

"What if we devise a new strategy? We spread apart so it's not so easy to shoot us?"

When it is time to work — work!

At an automotive industry convention in Las Vegas for car dealers and vendors I watched as one vendor, Scott (also known as Lasso Man), bobbed and weaved to avoid fork-lifts, extension cords, and workers who packed up the convention. Scott worked to the bitter end after three exhausting days.

Be happy — and hire happy people

If someone is so critical to your team that you keep them on board even though they are miserable, hide them in the back. They should never interact with customers. There is no excuse to have unpleasant people representing your company and driving away customers.

At the same automotive convention that I mentioned a moment ago, I saw another vendor, Brent, who travels 250+ days a year — working all day in his booth, even after teaching a workshop. Afterward, he networked and met with clients when the convention day ended. During and after all the hard work, he was enjoyable to talk with and never stopped smiling. He probably sleeps with a big smile on his face. He is just a happy guy.

Find other reasons or other markets to buy your stuff

A wallpaper cleaning solution became playdough — probably an accidental discovery. Here's a better example: you, a business owner, probably bought this book to read for yourself. Buy a copy for all of your employees and have them read Chapter 5 immediately.

7 Machine Gun Fire Tips

1 - I've been to restaurants where I place an order and pay with a credit card. Unbelievably, they ask my name so they can call me when my order is ready. If a customer hands you their credit card or some other form of identification, don't ask their name. It's right there in your hand.

2 - Smile. It's easy and free.

3 - When you say, "Can I put you on hold?" wait for a response before putting someone on hold.

4 - Smile while speaking on the phone. Your customer will hear the difference.

5 - Don't answer the phone with, "How may I direct your call?" I don't have a clue, I don't work there. How about you politely find out what I need and direct me to the right place — since you are the one getting paid to work there?

6 - Never say, "That is our policy," in response to, "Why?" Everyone hates that answer.

7 - Now, go to KennyTalks.com and get those extra resources, because you and I both know you'll forget — as people do.

Endnotes

1   Wired For Story, by Lisa Cron

2   The Irresistible Power of Storytelling as a Strategic Business Tool, by Harrison Monarth, Harvard Business Review, March 11, 2014

3   Speaker–listener neural coupling underlies successful communication, by Greg J. Stephens, Lauren J. Silbert, and Uri Hasson, Proceedings of the National Academy of Sciences, July 26, 2010

4   Storytelling program helps change medical students' perspectives on dementia, Science Daily, June 18, 2013

5   The Stories Behind 10 Famous Product Placements, by Stacy Conradt, Mental Floss

6   news.investors.com

7   http://www.copyblogger.com/the-greatest-sales-letter-of-all-time

8   Stealth Technology, by Larry Gilman via Encyclopedia of Espionage, Intelligence, and Security

9   SIFO Research International 2008

10   December 2011 by Epsilon 2011 Channel Preference Study

11   December 2011 by Epsilon Targeting Data from the "2011 Channel Preference Study"

12   December 2011 by Epsilon 2011 Channel Preference Study

13   Using Neuroscience to Understand the Role of Direct Mail - Millward Brown: Case Study 2009

14   USPS Data, reported in Direct Mail News 2/11

15   National Retail Federation Top 100 Retailers Chart

16   Costco CEO Craig Jelinek Leads the Cheapest, Happiest Company in the World, by Brad Stone, Bloomberg Business, June 6, 2013

17   Costco's Surprisingly Large-Circulation Magazine, by J. Max Robins, Content Marketing Insider, March 6, 2015

18   What the Rich Are Reading Biggest Surprises: Costco Connection and AARP's Magazine, by Mike Chapman, Adweek, April 26, 2011

19   High on H.O.G., GS, June 2014

20   Forbes Greatest Business Stories of All Time, by Daniel Gross, 1997

21   United Nations, Wikipedia

22   United Nations website, History of United Nations; Allies of World War II, Wikipedia

23   How to Unleash the Power of Strategic Partnerships, by Phil Khor, RecruitLoop

24   The Barista Principle — Starbucks and the Rise of Relational Capital, by Ranjay Gulati, Sarah Huffman, and Gary L. Neilson

25   http://www.nielsen.com/us/en/insights/news/2013/under-the-influence-consumer-trust-in-advertising.html

26   The Elements of Persuasion: Use Storytelling to Pitch Better, Sell Faster & Win More Business, by Richard Maxwell

27   Appreciation more important than pay, employees say, by Taryn Luna, The Boston Globe, November 17, 2013

28   Employee Confidence Remains Steady, Workplace Dynamics, August 28, 2015

29   Truffle Hog, Wikipedia

30   Record-breaking Rolls-Royce expects further gains from growing lineup, by Nick Gibbs, Automotive News Europe, March 5, 2015

31   Disney unleashes videos, CNN Money, November 11, 1999

32   No Easy Day: The Autobiography of a Navy SEAL, by Mark Owen

33   The 2014 customer service Hall of Fame, by Doug McIntyre, USA Today, July 19, 2014

34   Alaska Airlines and JetBlue Airways Continue to Rank Highest in Their Respective Segments, J.D. Power, May 13, 2015

35   The Tylenol Crisis: How Effective Public Relations Saved Johnson & Johnson, by Tamara Kaplan, The Pennsylvania State University

36   TechCrunch Network, July 23, 2009

37   2014 Wasting Time at Work Survey: Workers Are Wasting More Time Than Ever in 2014, by Aaron Gouveia, Salary.com

38   How Big of a Problem is Employee Theft and Fraud?, by Kay Foley, Incorp, January 10, 2014

39   Social Media as a Costly Time-Waster, by Alan Radding in wired FINANCE, Business Finance, Nov 1, 2012

40   2014 Wasting Time at Work Survey: Workers Are Wasting More Time Than Ever in 2014, by Aaron Gouveia, Salary.com

41   Americans and Text Messaging, by Aaron Smith, PewResearchCenter, September 19, 2011

42   The Radicati Group Releases "Email Statistics Report, 2015-2019," by the Radicati Team, The Radicati Group, Inc., March 2, 2015

43   Source: Attention Span Statistics, Statistic Brain Research Institute, April 2nd, 2015

44   United Breaks Guitars, Wikipedia

45   Your Call Is Important to Us. Please Stay Awake., by Ken Belson, New York Times, June 26, 2006

46   Under the Influence: Consumer Trust in Advertising, Nielson, September 17, 2003

47   Local Consumer Review Survey, BrightLocal, 2015

48   Lee Resource Inc.

49   The Customer Experience Index, 2012 — Forrester

50   Fascinate: Your 7 Triggers to Persuasion and Captivation, by Sally Hogshead

51   Joshie The Giraffe — A Remarkable Story About Customer Delight!, by Andy Hanselman, CustomerThink, May 18, 2012

52   https://www.cia.gov/about-cia/todays-cia/what-we-do

53   History of the CIA, Central Intelligence Agency

54   Broken Windows Broken Business, by Michael Levine

55   Einstein's Cosmos, by Michio Kaku